PRAYING
GOD'S
PROMISES

PRAYING GOD'S PROMISES

Victory House, Inc.
Tulsa, Oklahoma

Praying God's Promises
Copyright © 1998 by K. & C. International, Inc.
ISBN 0-932081-64-9 (Mass-market Paperback)
Published by Victory House, Inc.
P.O. Box 700238
Tulsa, Oklahoma 74170
(918) 747-5009

CONTENTS

PART 1

◆

ALL GOD'S PROMISES

1

Believing and Receiving God's Promises

*So then faith cometh by hearing, and
hearing by the word of God. (Rom. 10:17)*

God's Promises Are Trustworthy

There are literally hundreds of promises in
the Word of God, and each one of them is worthy
of implicit trust. What does this mean? If we are
to trust the promises of God implicitly, what does
that trust entail?

Trust, as it is defined by Webster, is ". . .
assured reliance on the character, ability, strength,
or truth of someone or something." To trust
God's promises, therefore, means that we rely
with assurance on God's character, ability, strength,
and truth as it is revealed to us in His Word.

Trust Christ for Salvation

The first condition we must meet in order to
trust the promises of God is to trust Christ for
salvation. When this happens, we know it,
because God's Word clearly states, "These things
have I written unto you that believe on the name
of the Son of God; that ye may know that ye have
eternal life, and that ye may believe on the name
of the Son of God" (1 John 5:13).

The promises of God open the doors to
salvation for us. Many of us were saved in

response to the faith that rose in our hearts when we heard God's promises being declared. Some of the promises related to salvation are:

> *But as many as received him, to them gave he power to become the sons of God, even to them that believe on his name. (John 1:12)*

> *For God so loved the world, that he gave his only begotten Son, that whosoever believeth in him should not perish, but have everlasting life. (John 3:16)*

> *Therefore if any man be in Christ, he is a new creature: old things are passed away; behold, all things are become new. (2 Cor. 5:17)*

> *For by grace are ye saved through faith; and that not of yourselves: it is the gift of God: Not of works, lest any man should boast. (Eph. 2:8-9)*

Each of the above Scriptures are salvation promises. When they are proclaimed to the heart of an unbeliever, faith is imparted that enables the unsaved to believe and receive God's blessed promise of salvation. When this happens, a marvelous miracle of personal transformation takes place.

The same process occurs when we listen carefully to any promise of God. His promises are worthy of trust because He is our faithful Father. When we know God's Word, we learn His promises, and faith to appropriate His promises is imparted to us in the manner Paul outlines: "So then faith comes by hearing, and hearing by the word of God" (Rom. 10:17, NKJV).

This phenomenon goes into operation whenever we hear any promise of God. The promise is proclaimed, and faith comes to back it up. Then we choose to believe and receive it. We claim the promise through prayer. Praying God's promises, therefore, is claiming God's promises. Believing God's promises is receiving God's promises.

A Multitude of Promises

Our inheritance, as believers in Jesus Christ and His Word, is a treasure of extensive worth. One of the promises from God's Word gives us insight into the inheritance we've already received: "Blessed be the God and Father of our Lord Jesus Christ, who hath blessed us with all spiritual blessings in heavenly places in Christ" (Eph. 1:3). God, our loving and giving Father, has already blessed us with all spiritual blessings in heavenly places in Christ! What a promise this is! It has already happened. We are already blessed, and each of God's promises is a particular treasure in the inheritance we've received from His hands. All spiritual blessings are already ours!

The Word of God promises so many things to us. Some of those blessings/promises are as follows: abundance, victory, hope, faith, peace, joy, growth, righteousness, wisdom, power, protection, eternal life, revival, rest, faith, trust, stability, strength, love, the Holy Spirit, patience, kindness, goodness, prosperity, health, peace, security, deliverance, dominion, authority, truth, forgiveness, and countless other gifts from the hands of God.

The following sections discuss some of these promises in more detail. When we examine the Scriptures from a promise-receiving perspective, we find new promises on almost every page. It is important to know that each of these promises are for us, God's children, to believe and receive, and we claim these promises through prayer.

The New Birth

We are born again when we trust Christ for salvation. The Scriptures provide us with many promises which back up the new birth that is available to everyone who believes.

> *That if thou shalt confess with thy mouth the Lord Jesus, and shalt believe in thine heart that God hath raised him from the dead, thou shalt be saved. For with the heart man believeth unto righteousness; and with the mouth confession is made unto salvation. (Rom. 10:9-10)*

> *Verily, verily, I say unto you, He that heareth my word, and believeth on him that sent me, hath everlasting life, and shall not come into condemnation; but is passed from death unto life. (John 5:24)*

> *Jesus answered and said unto him, Verily, verily, I say unto thee, Except a*

*man be born again, he cannot see the
kingdom of God. (John 3:3)*

These five promises from the Word of God
assure us that the new birth is available to all
who will believe. Notice how the process begins
with the hearing of God's Word. "He that
heareth my word, and believeth on him that sent
me, hath everlasting life" (John 5:24). We are
"born again, . . . by the word of God, which
liveth and abideth for ever" (1 Pet. 1:23). First,
the Word, then the faith.

To receive God's promises we must believe
God's promises.

The Power of Faith

Believing and receiving all of God's promises
is, after salvation, the most essential step we must
take in learning how to pray the promises. Faith is
the key ingredient for, as the Scriptures tell us, ". . .
without faith it is impossible to please him: for he
that cometh to God must believe that he is, and
that he is a rewarder of them that diligently seek
him" (Heb. 11:6). It is impossible to please God
without faith.

When we come to Him in prayer, we must
believe in Him, and we must also believe that He
is ready to reward our faith. Jesus said, ". . . your
Father knoweth what things ye have need of,
before ye ask him" (Matt. 6:8). This promise,
along with the one we find in Philippians 4:19:
"But my God shall supply all your need according
to his riches in glory by Christ Jesus," show us

that God knows our needs and He will meet our needs. Our heavenly Father wants to bless us!

As we learn to pray God's promises we must remember: "Faith is the substance of things hoped for, the evidence of things not seen" (Heb. 11:1). Praying the promises becomes effective when we pray with faith. Look at what Jesus said:

> *For verily I say unto you, If ye have faith as a grain of mustard seed, ye shall say unto this mountain, Remove hence to yonder place, and it shall remove; and nothing shall be impossible unto you.* (Matt. 17:20)

> *Have faith in God. For verily I say unto you, That whosoever shall say unto this mountain, Be thou removed, and be thou cast into the sea; and shall not doubt in his heart, but shall believe that those things which he saith shall come to pass; he shall have whatsoever he saith. Therefore I say unto you, What things soever ye desire, when ye pray, believe that ye receive them, and ye shall have them.* (Mark 11:22-24)

These prayer promises are directly from the lips of our Master, Jesus Christ. Notice how He elevates the powerful role of faith in prayer. According to our Savior, nothing is impossible to a person of faith. If we believe the promises of God when we pray them, Jesus says that we shall receive them. Indeed, all things are possible to a believer who trusts the promises of God.

Faith is a force that can move mountains, bring answers to our prayers, and help us to see new dimensions of life and victory in our daily lives and prayers. "For we walk by faith, not by sight" (2 Cor. 5:7).

The vehicle in which faith is conveyed to the human heart is the Word of God. We must never lose sight of this reality. ". . . faith cometh by hearing, and hearing by the word of God" (Rom. 10:17). The more we allow the Word to have its way in our lives the more our faith will grow and multiply. We need to saturate ourselves with the Word of God in meditation, worship, and prayer. This gives life to the promises of God.

The Power of the Word of God

We have already pointed out that God's Word is alive. In fact, it ". . . liveth and abideth for ever" (1 Pet. 1:23). It is alive and it is powerful.

> *By the word of the Lord were the heavens made; and all the host of them by the breath of his mouth. (Ps. 33:6)*

> *He sent his word, and healed them, and delivered them from their destructions. (Ps. 107:20)*

> *The entrance of thy words giveth light; it giveth understanding unto the simple. (Ps. 119:130)*

The power of God's Word is unlimited. As the above promises reveal, it is a creative power that imparts healing, life, understanding, and deliverance. Knowing the Word of God, and believing its precious promises, are the keys to faith and life. Jesus said, "Man shall not live by bread alone, but by every word that proceedeth out of the mouth of God" (Matt. 4:4).

Praying the promises of God puts the Word of God into powerful action in our lives. Praying the promises of God, in faith, is receiving the promises of God.

The Power of the Blood of Jesus

The blood of Jesus is "the scarlet thread" that is woven throughout the Scriptures. It is one major theme of the Bible. The infinite power of the blood of Jesus is declared in many Bible promises.

> *Much more then, being now justified by his blood, we shall be saved from wrath through him.* (Rom. 5:9)

> *The blood of Jesus Christ his Son cleanseth us from all sin.* (1 John 1:7)

> *In whom [Jesus Christ] we have redemption through his blood, the forgiveness of sins, according to the riches of his grace.* (Eph. 1:7)

Through the blood of Christ, we are able to partake of the promises of God, because His blood provides us with remission of all our sins, redemption, forgiveness, cleansing, and justification (a state of being just as if we'd never sinned). Through the blood of Jesus, we are able to draw near to God in prayer and worship, and we are able to receive all the promises He has for us. The blood of Jesus also helps us to defeat the enemy, as the promise of Scripture declares:

> *And they overcame him by the blood of the Lamb, and by the word of their testimony; and they loved not their lives unto the death. (Rev. 12:11)*

The Power of the Holy Spirit

The power of faith emanating from the Word of God, protected by the blood of Jesus and empowered by the Holy Spirit, fulfills the promises of God in our lives. Many people seem unaware of these sources of tremendous power that are available to us. It is the promises of God that reveal their power to us.

> *But if the Spirit of him that raised up Jesus from the dead dwell in you, he that raised up Christ from the dead shall also quicken your mortal bodies by his Spirit that dwelleth in you. (Rom. 8:11)*

> *But ye shall receive power, after that the Holy Ghost is come upon you: and ye shall be witnesses unto me both in Jerusalem, and in all Judaea, and in*

*Samaria, and unto the uttermost part of the
earth. (Acts 1:8)*

*And, behold, I send the promise of my
Father upon you: but tarry ye in the city of
Jerusalem, until ye be endued with power
from on high. (Luke 24:49)*

Each of these verses is a promise from the
Father, and Jesus refers to the Holy Spirit as "the
promise of my Father" (Luke 24:49).   Indeed,
whenever the Word of God is proclaimed, the
power of the blood of Jesus and the power of the
Holy Spirit are in operation, because the three
are indivisible.   When we pray the promises,
therefore, we are letting the power of the Holy
Spirit, the blood of Jesus, and the Word of God
loose in our lives. The result is absolute victory!

*For whatsoever is born of God over-
cometh the world: and this is the victory
that overcometh the world, even our faith.
(1 John 5:4)*

The Power of Grace

God's grace is greater than all our sin. His
grace (a gift of unmerited favor) gives us the
power of faith, the Word, the blood of Jesus, and
the Holy Spirit. It's not that we deserve these
sources of tremendous power, it's simply that God
loves us so much that He wants to reward our
faith by blessing us, protecting us, and meeting all
our needs.

Let's look at two of God's promises regarding grace:

> *For the Lord God is a sun and shield: the Lord will give grace and glory: no good thing will he withhold from them that walk uprightly.* (Ps. 84:11)

> *The Lord hath been mindful of us: he will bless us; he will bless the house of Israel; he will bless the house of Aaron. He will bless them that fear the Lord, both small and great.* (Ps. 115:12-13)

Though the latter promise in this list does not specifically mention the word grace, it directly pertains to grace because grace is God's loving favor at work in our lives. God will bless us, protect us, give us His favor, and He will not withhold any good thing from those who love and trust Him and believe the promises of His Word.

> *Let us therefore come boldly unto the throne of grace, that we may obtain mercy, and find grace to help in time of need.* (Heb. 4:16)

The Power of the Name of Jesus

Jesus said, "And whatsoever ye shall ask in my name, that will I do, that the Father may be glorified in the Son. If ye shall ask any thing in my name, I will do it" (John 14:13-15). If we ask *anything* in the name of Jesus, He promises He will bring it to pass in our lives. This is prevailing prayer. It is power in prayer, and it stems directly from believing and receiving the promises of God. The Lord's commandment: "Ask any thing in my name." The Lord's promise: *"I will do it."*

He also said, "Whatsoever ye shall ask the Father in my name, he will give it you. Hitherto have ye asked nothing in my name: ask, and ye shall receive, that your joy may be full" (John 16:23-24). The name of Jesus is all-powerful. It is above every name. The name of Jesus speaks to us of the power and authority of God. It assures us that He will fulfill His promises to us. Everything His name represents will bring God's answers to our needs.

When Jesus told His followers to pray in His name, He was giving us the "power of attorney" to represent Him — and all He possesses — by praying in His name. To pray in the name of Jesus is to pray in the full realization of who He is, what He stands for, what He is able to do, and what He wants. We are representing Him when we are praying in His name, and so we must be sure that our prayers are in agreement with Him and His Word.

That kind of praying brings results because it is praying in accord with the will of God as it is revealed by the promises of His Word. The Apostle John wrote, "And this is the confidence that we have in him, that, if we ask any thing according to his will, he heareth us: And if we know that he hear us, whatsoever we ask, we know that we have the petitions that we desired of him" (1 John 5:14-15).

The Power of Prayer

The Bible makes it clear that God wants His people to pray. "Rejoice evermore. Pray without ceasing. In every thing give thanks: for this is the will of God in Christ Jesus concerning you" (1 Thess. 5:16-18). Incessant, rejoicing, thankful prayer — this is God's will for each of us, and praying His promises unleashes the power of prayer in our lives.

God answers prayers that are built upon His promises, because His promises are His will for us. We have already pointed out that praying God's promises is praying His will. This kind of powerful praying brings miraculous results.

Through the Prophet Isaiah God promises, "And it shall come to pass, that before they call, I will answer; and while they are yet speaking, I will hear" (Isa. 65:24). God hears and answers prayers that are based upon His promises to us.

Jesus confirms this to our hearts in His Sermon on the Mount: "Ask, and it shall be given you; seek, and ye shall find; knock, and it shall be opened unto you: For every one that asketh receiveth; and he that seeketh findeth, and to him that knocketh it shall be opened" (Matt. 7:7-8).

Some other promises of answered prayer are listed below:

> *Call unto me, and I will answer thee, and shew thee great and mighty things, which thou knowest not. (Jer. 33:3)*

> *And whatsoever we ask, we receive of him, because we keep his commandments, and do those things that are pleasing in his sight. (1 John 3:22)*

> *The Lord is nigh unto all them that call upon him, to all that call upon him in truth. He will fulfil the desire of them that fear him: he also will hear their cry, and will save them. (Ps. 145:18-19)*

God wants us to call to Him. He wants us to pray to Him in secret. He wants us to keep His commandments. He wants us to call upon Him in truth and to fear Him, and He wants us to delight ourselves in Him.

The Power of Abiding

To abide means to stay put, to endure without yielding, and to practice patience. Abiding in Christ is the safest of all places to be. If we abide in Him, with our feet firmly planted on His promises, wonderful things will happen in our lives as a result of our prayers.

First and foremost, Jesus calls us: "Abide in me, and I in you. As the branch cannot bear fruit of itself, except it abide in the vine; no more can ye, except ye abide in me. I am the vine, ye are the branches: He that abideth in me, and I in him, the same bringeth forth much fruit: for without me ye can do nothing. If a man abide not in me, he is cast forth as a branch, and is withered; and men gather them and cast them into the fire, and they are burned. If ye abide in me, and my words abide in you, ye shall ask what ye will, and it shall be done unto you" (John 15:4-7).

Stay put in Jesus, endure without yielding to the distractions of the enemy, and keep on keeping on. "Let the word of Christ dwell in you richly in all wisdom" (Col. 3:16).

The Power of the Promises

R.A. Torrey writes, "We go into God's presence with the thing we desire. Next, we ask ourselves this question: Is there any promise in God's Word regarding what we desire? We look into the Word of God and find the promise. Then all we have to do is to present that promise to God. For example, we say, 'Heavenly Father, we desire the Holy Spirit. You say in Your Word, "If ye then, being evil, know how to give good gifts unto your children, how much more shall your heavenly Father give the Holy Spirit to them that ask him?", and again in Acts 2:39, that "the promise is unto you, and to your children, and to all that are afar off, even as many as the Lord our God shall call." I have been called; I am saved; and here in Your Word is Your promise. So please fill me now with the Holy Spirit.'

"We then take 1 John 5:14-15, and say, 'Father, this is the confidence I have in You, that, if I ask anything according to Your will — and know that this is according to Your will — You hear me, and, if I know that You hear me, I know that I have the petition that I have asked of You.' Then we stand on God's promise and say, 'It is mine,' and it will be. The only way to have a faith that prevails in prayer is to study your Bible, know the promises, and present them to God when you pray."

In these two short paragraphs Torrey gives us the heart of the matter. How do we pray God's promises? First, we study God's Word. Second, we let faith arise in our hearts. Third, we believe and receive God's promises. The next step, which we outline in the following section, is to personalize the promises as we present them to God in prayer.

Prevailing faith comes from the prevailing promises of God's Word. Standing on those promises and praying them in faith is prevailing prayer. Find God's promises. Study God's promises. Believe God's promises. Receive God's promises. Live God's promises, and pray God's promises.

Praying the promises of God enables us to receive the answers to our prayers even as we pray.

2

Laying Claim to Our Inheritance

Is not my word like as a fire? saith the Lord; and like a hammer that breaketh the rock in pieces? (Jer. 23:29)

Children of the King

As a result of the new birth we have been born into a royal family. The King of kings and Lord of lords has adopted us into His family, and now we enjoy all the rights and privileges associated with royalty. We have received a royal inheritance.

The Bible says, "In whom also we have obtained an inheritance, being predestinated according to the purpose of him who worketh all things after the counsel of his own will: That we should be to the praise of his glory, who first trusted in Christ" (Eph. 1:11-12). The promises of God form and reveal the inheritance we have received from our heavenly Father.

C. H. Spurgeon wrote, "Every promise of Scripture is a writing of God which may be pleaded before Him with this reasonable request: 'Do as Thou hast said.' The Creator will not cheat His creature who depends upon His truth; and, far more, the Heavenly Father will not break His word to His own child. 'Remember the word unto Thy servant, on which Thou hast caused me to hope,' is most prevalent pleading. It is a double argument: It is Thy Word, wilt Thou not keep it? Why hast Thou spoken of it if Thou wilt not make it good? Thou hast caused me to hope in it; wilt Thou disappoint the hope which Thou hast Thyself begotten in me?"

The promises of God are our inheritance as children of the King, and because this is true, we can lay claim to those promises through prayer.

Personal Promises

E.M. Bounds writes, "God's promises are always personal and specific. They are not general, indefinite, vague. They do not have to do with multitudes and classes of people in a mass, but are directed to individuals. They deal with persons. Each believer can claim the promise as his own. God deals with each one personally. So that every saint can put the promises to the test. 'Prove me now herewith, saith the Lord.' No need of generalizing, nor of being lost in vagueness. The praying saint has the right to put his hand upon the promise and claim it as his own, one made especially to him, and one intended to embrace all his needs, present and future."

When we say yes to God's promises, God says yes to us. When we say amen to God's promises, God says amen to us. "For all the promises of God in Him are Yes, and in Him Amen, to the glory of God through us" (2 Cor. 1:20, NKJV).

God's promises are for our personal consumption. They are for us as individuals. God wants us to claim them as our own. They are our privileges as children of the great King.

Claiming the Promises

In the newspapers and on television we often hear of people who are entitled to claim inheritances that belong to them but they do not know about them. In these cases, the ones who are holding the inheritances do not have a way to get in touch with the beneficiaries who deserve to receive what is coming to them because the beneficiaries cannot be located. The problem is a lack of knowledge, a lack of understanding. This is often true of believers as well. The unsearchable riches of Christ are available to each of us, but unfortunately some folks don't realize that these riches are available to us. Like the people who have inheritances awaiting them, they are unable to lay claim to what is rightfully theirs because they do not know that it is their privilege to do so.

When the beneficiaries of the unknown inheritances discover what is rightfully theirs, they rejoice with great excitement, and often they stop whatever they're doing in order to go and claim their unexpected blessings. They feel as if they've won a sweepstakes, and sometimes their inheritance changes almost everything in their lives. The same kinds of things happen when believers discover their inheritance as children of the King. Knowing and trusting God's promises changes everything in our lives.

Paul, when he prayed for the Ephesians, outlined our inheritance as follows: "That the God of our Lord Jesus Christ, the Father of glory, may give unto you the spirit of wisdom and revelation in the knowledge of him: the eyes of your understanding being enlightened; that ye may know what is the hope of his calling, and what the riches of the glory of his inheritance in the saints, and what is the exceeding greatness of his power to us-ward who believe, according to the working of his mighty power" (Eph. 1:17-20).

Our rightful inheritance as believers in Jesus Christ includes the spirit of wisdom and revelation in the knowledge of God, enlightened spiritual understanding, the hope of His calling, the riches of His glory, and the exceeding greatness of His power. These are ours to claim.

When the realization of the extent of this inheritance dawns upon us, it causes us to rejoice with Paul who wrote, "Blessed be the God and Father of our Lord Jesus Christ, who hath blessed us with all spiritual blessings in heavenly places in Christ" (Eph. 1:3). All spiritual blessings in Christ are already ours! All we have to do is to lay claim to them, and we do this through prayer.

Firm Ground for Prayer

E. M. Bounds writes, "How large are the promises made to the saint! How great the promises given to poor, hungry-hearted, lost sinners, ruined by the fall! And prayer has arms sufficient to encompass them all, and prove them. How great the encouragement to all souls, these promises of God! How firm the ground on which to rest our faith! How stimulating to prayer! What firm ground on which to base our pleas in praying!"

Yes, the promises of God are a firm ground to stand upon as we pray to the Father. When we're standing on the promises, as the old hymn declares, we cannot fail. God cannot lie. He is absolutely trustworthy.

God promises much more to you than you may realize. The Word tells us, "Eye has not seen, nor ear heard, nor have entered into the heart of man the things which God has prepared for those who love Him. But God has revealed them to us through His Spirit" (1 Cor. 2:9-10, NKJV).

God Said It — I Believe It!

"Thus God, determining to show more abundantly the heirs of promise the immutability of His counsel, confirmed it by an oath, that by two immutable things, in which it is impossible for God to lie, we might have strong consolation, who have fled for refuge to lay hold of the hope set before us. This hope we have as an anchor of the soul, both sure and steadfast, and which enters the Presence behind the veil" (Heb. 6:17-19, NKJV).

The fact is that God cannot lie. His very nature is truth. We are the heirs of His promise, and He wants to bless us ever more abundantly. The hope we have stems from His promises to us, and these promises are sure and steadfast. They are an anchor for our souls.

God said to Abraham, "Surely blessing I will
bless you, and multiplying I will multiply you"
(Heb. 6:14, NKJV). "And so, after he had patiently
endured, he obtained the promise" (Heb. 6:15,
NKJV). It is the same for each of us.

If God said it, you can count upon it.

Meditate on God's Promises

"The word is near you, in your mouth and in
your heart (that is, the word of faith which we
preach): that if you confess with your mouth the
Lord Jesus and believe in your heart that God has
raised Him from the dead, you will be saved. For
with the heart one believes unto righteousness,
and with the mouth confession is made unto
salvation" (Rom. 10:8-10, NKJV).

When we meditate on God's promises in our
mind and heart, our faith to lay hold of our inheritance multiplies. When we speak God's promises
to others they are encouraged, strengthened, and
comforted. When we pray God's promises we
receive God's answers.

> *Blessed is the man that walketh not in*
> *the counsel of the ungodly, nor standeth in*
> *the way of sinners, nor sitteth in the seat of*
> *the scornful. But his delight is in the law of*
> *the Lord; and in his law doth he meditate*
> *day and night. And he shall be like a tree*
> *planted by the rivers of water, that bringeth*
> *forth his fruit in his season; his leaf also*
> *shall not wither; and whatsoever he doeth*
> *shall prosper. (Ps. 1:1-3)*

Each of us needs to reprogram how we think. We need to get our thinking in agreement with God's Word. We need to accentuate the positive and eliminate the negative in our thinking. The way to do this is to remind ourselves repeatedly of the promises of God through meditation and prayer.

As we memorize, reflect upon, think, and dwell upon the promises of God, our minds will be renewed and our lives transformed. (See Rom. 12:1-2.) God's Word will become the framework on which our prayers are built. A believer is victorious at all times. A believer knows that God always honors His Word.

The Power of the Tongue

"Death and life are in the power of the tongue, and those who love it will eat its fruit" (Prov. 18:21, NKJV). No one likes to eat rotten fruit, because it is not good for you and it tastes very bad. The wonderful words of life — God's precious promises — are life and health and victory, and as we learn to embrace these truths and claim them as our rightful inheritance we will eat the fruit of life and health and victory. These are the good fruits that are produced when we learn to meditate upon and pray the promises of God.

"Let us draw near with a true heart in full assurance of faith, having our hearts sprinkled from an evil conscience and our bodies washed with pure water. Let us hold fast the confession of our hope without wavering, for He who promised is faithful" (Heb. 10:22-23, NKJV).

Let us remember what the Word tells us: "Whoso keepeth his mouth and his tongue keepeth his soul from troubles" (Prov. 21:23). What we think with our minds and hearts eventually comes forth in our words and deeds. This is why it is vitally important for us to think God's thoughts and to pray His promises. "For as he thinketh in his heart, so is he" (Prov. 23:7).

Jesus reminds us, "A good man out of the good treasure of his heart brings forth good; and an evil man out of the evil treasure of his heart brings forth evil. For out of the abundance of the heart his mouth speaks" (Luke 6:45, NKJV).

Affirm God's Word in Prayer

Affirming God's Word strengthens our faith and it enables us to lay claim to our inheritance as believers. Each day we need to affirm God's Word in prayer by praying His promises. This actualizes them in our daily lives. God's promises are not simply nice theories; they are realities for us to receive.

As we listen for God's voice in prayer, we will hear Him reminding us of His promises, and this lifts us above the circumstances, even when things may not be going as well as we would like. At such times, we need to remember God's Word: "Faith is the substance of things hoped for, the evidence of things not seen" (Heb. 11:1).

As we pray the promises, we are affirming God's truths and applying them to our situation. Jesus said, "Whatsoever ye shall bind on earth shall be bound in heaven: and whatsoever ye shall loose on earth shall be loosed in heaven" (Matt. 18:18). This is agreeing with God in prayer, and it is affirming His power in our lives.

We need to bind ourselves to the will of God and the Word of God, and in so doing, we will have the power to bind all forces of negativity and evil that may endeavor to discourage or defeat us. Likewise, as we affirm God's Word through prayer, we loose ourselves from any bondage or sin that may hold us back.

Jesus said, "If ye continue in my word, then are ye my disciples indeed; And ye shall know the truth, and the truth shall make you free" (John 8:31-32).

Affirming Who We Are in Christ

Several promises from the Word of God reveal our true identity to us. When we know these truths, we will no longer ask ourselves, "Who am I?" Our search for our personal identity is fulfilled in these promises. Two of those passages are cited below:

> *Therefore if any man be in Christ, he is a new creature: old things are passed away; behold, all things are become new. (2 Cor. 5:17)*

> *He has delivered us from the power of darkness and conveyed us into the kingdom of the Son of His love, in whom*

> *we have redemption through His blood, the*
> *forgiveness of sins. (Col. 1:13-14, NKJV)*

In Christ, we are a new creation. The old
things are gone, and all things have become new
to us.

In Christ, we have been delivered from the
power of darkness. We have been conveyed into
the Kingdom of Jesus Christ.

In Christ, we have been redeemed and
forgiven of all our sins.

In Christ, we have access to all the treasures
of wisdom and knowledge.

In Christ, we are complete.

These are the affirmations we need to be
saying to ourselves. These are the thoughts we
need to be thinking. These are the promises we
need to be praying.

Jesus Is Everything to Us

Jesus said, "I am the way, the truth, and the
life: no man cometh unto the Father, but by me"
(John 14:6). As we personalize this promise in
prayer and affirmation, we say, "Jesus is *my* way,
my truth, and *my* life." This is a powerful, faith-
building affirmation.

As we pray, it is important to lay claim to
our rightful inheritance as children of the King by
reflecting on who Jesus is to us, individually and
personally. For example, we would pray: "Lord
Jesus, you are my Shepherd. I shall not want.
You lead me. (See Ps. 23.) You are my Good

Shepherd. (See John 10:14.) You are the door that opens an entirely new life to me. (See John 10:9-11.) You are my fortress, and my sure defense. (See Ps. 89:18.)

"You are my rock of refuge, my high tower, my shield, and my buckler. (See Ps. 18:30.) You are the Word that became flesh and dwelt among us. (See John 1:14.) You are the Word of Life. (See 1 John 1:1.) You are Immanuel — God with me. (See Isa. 7:14.) You are my righteousness and the strength of my life. You are my light and my salvation; therefore, I have nothing to fear. (See Ps. 27:1.)

"I thank you that you are the first and the last, the Alpha and Omega. (See Rev. 1:8.) You are the Sun of righteousness. (See Mal. 4:2.) You are the fragrant Rose of Sharon and the fairest of ten thousand. You are the Lily of the Valley. (See Song of Solomon 2:1.) You are the bright and morning star. (See Rev. 22:16.) You are the light of the world, and in you there is no darkness at all. (See 1 John 1:5.)

"You are called Wonderful, Counselor, the Mighty God, the everlasting Father, and the Prince of Peace. (See Isa. 9:6.) You are the Holy One of Israel, the Lamb that was slain from the foundation of the world. (See Rev. 13:8.) At your name, every knee must bow and every tongue must confess that you are Lord to the glory of God the Father. (See Phil. 2:10.) You are the God in whom I live and move and have my being. (See Acts 17:28.) You meet all my needs." (See Phil. 4:19.)

This is a prayer of faith that coincides completely with the will of God for our lives. It is a model prayer in that it shows us how to pray the promises of God through personalization, affirming His Word, and claiming His promises. This form of prayer can be used with regard to any topic or concern we may sense a need to pray about. The last section of this book provides the believer with sample prayers concerning a variety of topics that are built directly from the promises of God.

Our position in Christ enables us to lay claim to all the promises of God, and His indwelling presence in our lives fulfills each of those promises to us. Christ dwells within us, and we are truly complete in Him. (See Col. 2:10.)

Personalizing the Promises of God

There are several questions to ask ourselves as we are gleaning personal truths from any passage of Scripture. Some appropriate questions include: What does the passage teach me about Jesus Christ? Is there any error in the passage for me to avoid? Is there any command in this passage for me to obey? Is there any example in this passage for me to follow? And most importantly, is there any promise in this passage for me to claim?

Your answers to these questions form the framework for effectual prayers based on the Word of God. James wrote, "The effective, fervent prayer of a righteous man avails much" (James 5:16, NKJV), and no prayer is more effective than one that lays hold of our royal inheritance by praying God's promises.

We don't pray God's promises in order to remind God of them. He already knows them and acts upon them faithfully. We pray God's promises so that we will remember them and act upon them. We pray God's promises so that our faith will grow. We pray God's promises so that we will receive divinely appointed answers to each of our prayers.

R.A. Torrey wrote, "If we are to receive from God all we ask from Him, Christ's words must abide in us. We must study His words and let them sink into our thoughts and heart. We must keep them in our memory, obey them constantly in our life, and let them shape and mold our daily life and our every act."

He went on, "This is really the method of abiding in Christ. It is through His words that Jesus imparts Himself to us. The words He speaks unto us, they are spirit and they are life (John 6:63). It is vain to expect power in prayer unless we meditate upon the words of Christ and let them sink deep and find a permanent abode in our hearts. There are many who wonder why they are so powerless in prayer. The very simple explanation of it all is found in their neglect of the words of Christ. They have not hidden His words in their hearts; His words do not abide in them. It is not by moments of mystical meditation and rapturous experiences that we learn to abide in Christ. It is by feeding upon His Word, His written word in the Bible, and looking to the Spirit to implant these words in our heart — to thus make them a living thing in our heart. If we thus let the words of Christ abide in us, they will stir us up to prayer. *They would be the mold in which our prayers are shaped.* And our prayers will necessarily be along the line of God's will and will prevail with Him. Prevailing prayer is almost an impossibility where there is neglect of the study of God's Word."

3

Prayer Promises From God's Word

*But we will give ourselves continually
to prayer, and to the ministry of the word.
(Acts 6:4)*

Obtaining the Promises

The Word of God promises us all good
things if we will believe and obey the Lord. As
we have pointed out, it promises us healing,
prosperity, guidance, revival, and victory. God
also promises us peace, health, wisdom, truth,
happiness, deliverance, protection, eternal life,
abundant life, freedom, and so many other
blessings. In order to obtain these promises we
need to know them, love them, believe them, live
them, and pray them.

Peter wrote, "Whereby are given unto us
exceeding great and precious promises: that by
these ye might be partakers of the divine nature,
having escaped the corruption that is in the world
through lust" (2 Pet. 1:4). The exceeding great and
precious promises of God have already been given
to us, and they enable us to partake of God's
nature and to escape the corruption of the world.

Obtaining the promises of God, however,
sometimes requires patience, as the Word points
out, "For ye have need of patience, that, after ye
have done the will of God, ye might receive the

promise. For yet a little while, and he that shall come will come, and will not tarry" (Heb. 10:36-37).

In order to obtain the promises of God we must be obedient to the Lord's commandments. "For if ye shall diligently keep all these commandments which I command you, to do them, to love the Lord your God, to walk in all his ways, and to cleave unto him; Then will the Lord drive out all these nations from before you, and ye shall possess greater nations and mightier than yourselves" (Deut. 11:22-23).

To obtain the promises we need faith. "But without faith it is impossible to please him: for he that cometh to God must believe that he is, and that he is a rewarder of them that diligently seek him" (Heb. 11:6).

To obtain the promises we must be strong and courageous. "Only be thou strong and very courageous, that thou mayest observe to do according to all the law, which Moses my servant commanded thee: turn not from it to the right hand or to the left, that thou mayest prosper withersoever thou goest" (Josh. 1:7).

To obtain the promises we must be active. "That ye be not slothful, but followers of them who through faith and patience inherit the promises" (Heb. 6:12).

To obtain the promises we must put God first. "But seek ye first the kingdom of God, and his righteousness; and all these things shall be added unto you" (Matt. 6:33).

Prayer is the avenue that takes us from the problem to the promise, from doubt to discovery, from the valley to the mountaintop, from discouragement to encouragement, from fear to faith, from despair to hope, from lies to truth, from confusion to wisdom, and from loss to gain. Praying God's promises brings life, peace, joy, and victory in every area of our lives.

The final section of the book applies the promises to common human needs and concerns. Included are brief teachings and promise-prayers for you to use. It is thrilling to know that God will bless you by His promises, through His promises, and with His promises.

"Therefore it is of faith, that it might be by grace; to the end the promise might be sure to all the seed; not to that only which is of the law, but to that also which is of the faith of Abraham; who is the father of us all" (Rom. 4:16).

What happens when people pray the promises? The following prayer promises give God's answers to this question.

He Protects Us

"The God of my rock; in him will I trust: he is my shield, and the horn of my salvation, my high tower, and my refuge, my saviour; thou savest me from violence. I will call on the Lord, who is worthy to be praised: so shall I be saved from mine enemies" (2 Sam. 22:3-4).

"Then shall ye call upon me, and ye shall go and pray unto me, and I will hearken unto you.

And ye shall seek me, and find me, when ye shall search for me with all your heart. And I will be found of you, saith the Lord: and I will turn away your captivity, and I will gather you from all the nations" (Jer. 29:12-14).

"Behold, I give unto you power to tread on serpents and scorpions, and over all the power of the enemy: and nothing shall by any means hurt you" (Luke 10:19).

"Now unto him that is able to keep you from falling, and to present you faultless before the presence of his glory with exceeding joy, To the only wise God our Saviour, be glory and majesty, dominion and power, both now and ever. Amen" (Jude 24-25).

He Hears Us

"In my distress I called upon the Lord, and cried to my God: and he did hear my voice out of his temple, and my cry did enter into his ears" (2 Sam. 22:7).

"Thus saith the Lord, the God of David thy father, I have heard thy prayer, I have seen thy tears: behold, I will heal thee" (2 Kings 20:5).

"He heareth the cry of the afflicted" (Job 34:28).

"But know that the Lord hath set apart him that is godly for himself: the Lord will hear when I call unto him" (Ps. 4:3).

"He forgetteth not the cry of the humble" (Ps. 9:12).

"Blessed be the Lord, because he hath heard the voice of my supplications" (Ps. 28:6).

"I sought the Lord, and he heard me, and delivered me from all my fears" (Ps. 34:4).

"In my distress I cried unto the Lord, and he heard me" (Ps. 120:1).

"The Lord is far from the wicked; but he heareth the prayer of the righteous" (Prov. 15:29).

"They shall call on my name, and I will hear them: I will say, It is my people: and they shall say, The Lord is my God" (Zech. 13:9).

"The eyes of the Lord are over the righteous, and his ears are open unto their prayers" (1 Pet. 3:12).

"And this is the confidence that we have in him, that, if we ask any thing according to his will, he heareth us" (1 John 5:14).

"And if we know that he hear us, whatsoever we ask, we know that we have the petitions that we desired of him" (1 John 5:15).

He Heals Us

"Thus saith the Lord, the God of David thy father, I have heard thy prayer, I have seen thy tears: behold, I will heal thee" (2 Kings 20:5).

"He shall call upon me, and I will answer him: I will be with him in trouble; I will deliver him, and honour him. With long life will I satisfy him, and shew him my salvation" (Ps. 91:15-16).

He Delivers Us

"I sought the Lord, and he heard me, and delivered me from all my fears" (Ps. 34:4).

"This poor man cried, and the Lord heard him, and saved him out of all his troubles" (Ps. 34:6).

"Offer unto God thanksgiving; and pay thy vows unto the most High: and call upon me in the day of trouble: I will deliver thee, and thou shalt glorify me" (Ps. 50:14-15).

"And it shall come to pass, that whosoever shall call on the name of the Lord shall be delivered" (Joel 2:32).

He Answers Our Prayers

"He shall call upon me, and I will answer him: I will be with him in trouble; I will deliver him, and honour him. With long life will I satisfy him, and shew him my salvation" (Ps. 91:15-16).

"Call unto me, and I will answer thee, and shew thee great and mighty things, which thou knowest not" (Jer. 33:3).

"Your Father knoweth what things ye have need of, before ye ask him" (Matt. 6:8).

"Ask, and it shall be given you; seek, and ye shall find; knock, and it shall be opened unto you: For every one that asketh receiveth; and he that seeketh findeth; and to him that knocketh it shall be opened" (Matt. 7:7-8).

"If ye then, being evil, know how to give good gifts unto your children, how much more shall your Father which is in heaven give good things to them that ask him?" (Matt. 7:11).

"Again I say unto you, That if two of you shall agree on earth as touching any thing that they shall ask, it shall be done for them of my Father which is in heaven. For where two or three are gathered together in my name, there am I in the midst of them" (Matt. 18:19-20).

"And all things, whatsoever ye shall ask in prayer, believing, ye shall receive" (Matt. 21:22).

"And Jesus answering saith unto them, Have faith in God. For verily I say unto you, That whosoever shall say unto this mountain, Be thou removed, and be thou cast into the sea; and shall not doubt in his heart, but shall believe that those things which he saith shall come to pass; he shall have whatsoever he saith. Therefore I say unto you, What things soever ye desire, when ye pray, believe that ye receive them, and ye shall have them" (Mark 11:22-24).

"But I know, that even now, whatsoever thou wilt ask of God, God will give it thee" (John 11:22).

"And whatsoever ye shall ask in my name, that will I do, that the Father may be glorified in the Son. If ye shall ask any thing in my name, I will do it" (John 14:13-14).

"If ye abide in me, and my words abide in you, ye shall ask what ye will, and it shall be done unto you" (John 15:7).

"Verily, verily, I say unto you, Whatsoever ye shall ask the Father in my name, he will give it you" (John 16:23).

"Hitherto have ye asked nothing in my name: ask, and ye shall receive, that your joy may be full" (John 16:24).

"For there is no difference between the Jew and the Greek: for the same Lord over all is rich unto all that call upon him" (Rom. 10:12).

"Now unto him that is able to do exceeding abundantly above all that we ask or think, according to the power that worketh in us, Unto him be glory in the church by Christ Jesus throughout all ages, world without end. Amen" (Eph. 3:20-21).

"Faithful is he that calleth you, who also will do it" (1 Thess. 5:24).

"Let us therefore come boldly unto the throne of grace, that we may obtain mercy, and find grace to help in time of need" (Heb. 4:16).

"But without faith it is impossible to please him: for he that cometh to God must believe that he is, and that he is a rewarder of them that diligently seek him" (Heb. 11:6).

"If any of you lack wisdom, let him ask of God, that giveth to all men liberally, and upbraideth not; and it shall be given him. But let him ask in faith, nothing wavering. For he that wavereth is like a wave of the sea driven with the wind and tossed" (James 1:5-6).

"Ye have not, because ye ask not" (James 4:2).

"The effectual fervent prayer of a righteous man availeth much" (James 5:16).

"And whatsoever we ask, we receive of him, because we keep his commandments, and do those things that are pleasing in his sight" (1 John 3:22).

"And if we know that he hear us, whatsoever we ask, we know that we have the petitions that we desired of him" (1 John 5:15).

He Will Give Us Long Life

"He shall call upon me, and I will answer him: I will be with him in trouble; I will deliver him, and honour him. With long life will I satisfy him, and shew him my salvation" (Ps. 91:15-16).

He Will Draw Near to Us

"The Lord is nigh unto all them that call upon him, to all that call upon him in truth" (Ps. 145:18).

"Draw nigh to God, and he will draw nigh to you" (James 4:8).

He Will Show Us Supernatural Truths

"Call unto me, and I will answer thee, and shew thee great and mighty things, which thou knowest not" (Jer. 33:3).

He Will Meet Our Needs

"Your Father knoweth what things ye have need of, before ye ask him" (Matt. 6:8).

"Ask, and it shall be given you; seek, and ye shall find; knock, and it shall be opened unto you: For every one that asketh receiveth; and he that

seeketh findeth; and to him that knocketh it shall
be opened" (Matt. 7:7-8).

"If ye then, being evil, know how to give
good gifts unto your children, how much more
shall your Father which is in heaven give good
things to them that ask him?" (Matt. 7:11).

"But my God shall supply all your need
according to his riches in glory by Christ Jesus"
(Phil. 4:19).

He Gives Us Power Over the Enemy

"Behold, I give unto you power to tread on
serpents and scorpions, and over all the power of
the enemy: and nothing shall by any means hurt
you" (Luke 10:19).

"Submit yourselves therefore to God. Resist
the devil, and he will flee from you" (James 4:7).

"And they overcame him by the blood of the
Lamb, and by the word of their testimony; and they
loved not their lives unto the death" (Rev. 12:11).

He Does Exceedingly, Abundantly
Beyond Our Expectations

"Now unto him that is able to do exceeding
abundantly above all that we ask or think, according
to the power that worketh in us, Unto him be
glory in the church by Christ Jesus throughout all
ages, world without end" (Eph. 3:20-21).

"Now unto him that is able to keep you from
falling, and to present you faultless before the
presence of his glory with exceeding joy, To the
only wise God our Saviour, be glory and majesty,

dominion and power, both now and ever. Amen" (Jude 24-25).

We, the believers in Jesus Christ, are the most fortunate people who ever walked the face of the earth. We are the happiest people who ever lived. We are the most victorious people in the world. It's because of the rich and precious promises of God. Promises that God wants us to claim as our own through faith and prayer.

> *For all the promises of God in him are yea, and in him Amen, unto the glory of God by us. (2 Cor. 1:20)*

4

The Steps to Take

*For all the promises of God in Him
are Yes, and in Him Amen, to the glory of
God through us. (2 Cor. 1:20, NKJV)*

This small steps-to-take section summarizes
the how-to process that is prerequisite to praying
God's promises. If the following steps are
adhered to, miraculous results will take place as a
result of your prayers.

Step 1 — Know God's Word

In the same way that food nourishes our
bodies, the Word of God provides nourishment
for our souls and spirits. Jesus said, "It is written,
That man shall not live by bread alone, but by
every word of God" (Luke 4:4).

To know God's Word, we must study the
Scriptures as Paul instructed Timothy to do:
"Study to shew thyself approved unto God, a
workman that needeth not to be ashamed, rightly
dividing the word of truth" (2 Tim. 2:15).

To know God's Word, we must memorize its
truths as the Psalmist pointed out, "Thy word
have I hid in mine heart, that I might not sin
against thee" (Ps. 119:11). Having the Word of
God firmly implanted in our hearts does keep us
from sin, because it is the sword of the Spirit that
is always able to slay the enemy. (See Eph. 6:17.)

Step 2 — Believe God's Word

Reading, as an intellectual exercise, may satisfy our mental curiosity and it may even provide entertainment for us. When it comes to the Word of God, however, our reading results in a far-more-wonderful purpose — it builds faith in our hearts.

Paul wrote, "So then faith cometh by hearing, and hearing by the word of God" (Rom. 10:17). As we read and study God's Word, therefore, we must be careful to search for all the promises God has made to us. Then we reach out in faith to trust those promises, fully believing that God will always honor His Word to us.

God keeps His Word. He does not lie. No matter how dismal circumstances might seem at times, we need to keep our focus clear: "It is of the Lord's mercies that we are not consumed, because his compassions fail not. They are new every morning: great is thy faithfulness. The Lord is my portion, saith my soul; therefore will I hope in him. The Lord is good unto them that wait for him, to the soul that seeketh him" (Lam. 3:22-25).

Step 3 — Receive God's Word

When a desirable gift is presented to us it is our responsibility to reach out and take it, to receive it into our own hands and lives. The same is true with the promises of God. They are for us. They are gifts from our Father in heaven who wants to bless His children more abundantly than many realize.

James writes, "Every good gift and every perfect gift is from above, and cometh down from the Father of lights, with whom is no variableness, neither shadow of turning" (James 1:17). Our God never changes and His promises are forever true.

In order to receive His promises, however, it is essential that we know what they are. As we read, study, memorize, and meditate upon God's Word, He brings the promises to life for us. We become amazed by all God wants to give to us.

"Eye hath not seen, nor ear heard, neither have entered into the heart of man, the things which God hath prepared for them that love him. But God hath revealed them unto us by his Spirit: for the Spirit searcheth all things, yea, the deep things of God" (1 Cor. 2:9-10). As God's promises come alive to us through the Spirit of God revealing them to us through His Word, we are able to receive them and apply them to our lives and prayers.

Step 4 — Personalize the Word

The Bible is more personal than any other book. It speaks to our hearts, because it is a message from our Father's heart to us. Therefore, it is appropriate for us to say, "Every promise is the Book is mine. Every promise is for *me*."

This realization enables us to claim God's promises to meet our every need. The religious art of the ancients depicts nearly every Bible story and Bible truth available to us. These paintings can be appreciated on a variety of levels, but it is only as we understand the artwork's personal significance to us as individuals that it has any impact in our personal lives.

For example, people may see pictures of the Crucifixion, or crucifixes hanging on a wall, but it is only as the realization dawns upon them that Jesus died for them that the images have any true meaning for them. This happens as the Spirit of God moves upon them and their spirit proclaims, "It was for *me* that He died. He was crucified for *me*." When this happens our lives are transformed.

In much the same way, when we personalize God's promises, we begin to see all of life from a different perspective — from the perspective of the spirit. "But the natural man receiveth not the things of the Spirit of God: for they are foolishness unto him: neither can he know them, because they are spiritually discerned" (1 Cor. 2:14).

Step 5 — Pray the Promises

Once you have immersed yourself in the Word of God and have allowed its truths to saturate deeply within your spirit, you are ready to walk by faith, not by sight. (See 2 Cor. 5:7.) Your study of the Word of God opens your eyes to the deeper truths of God, and those truths make you free. (See John 8:32.)

The spiritual freedom you enter into enables you to believe God's Word and to trust His promises implicitly. Your whole life becomes centered on the truths presented in this promise: "Trust in the Lord with all thine heart; and lean not unto thine own understanding. In all thy ways acknowledge him, and he shall direct thy paths" (Prov. 3:5-6).

Yes, God will lead you each step of the way, and as you begin to apply the truths of His Word through a personalized faith and a promise-focused prayer-life, you are fully prepared to enter into the most exciting of all forms of prayer — praying the promises. Why is this the most exciting form of prayer? Because it brings answers. It enables you to see the answers to your prayers while you are praying.

The Word of God promises us, "And this is the confidence that we have in him, that, if we ask any thing according to his will, he heareth us: And if we know that he hear us, whatsoever we ask, we know that we have the petitions that we desired of him" (1 John 5:14-15).

We can pray God's promises with confidence because we know that when we do so, we are praying according to the Father's will. The Word of God gives us the whole counsel of God, so when we pray His promises we are praying what He wants us to pray and believe. When we pray His Word, He hears us and answers us.

Step 6 — Answered Prayer

The Word of God speaks to every human need. Its truths apply to every aspect of our lives — physically, financially, familially, relationally, emotionally, mentally, sexually, vocationally, and spiritually. The Word of God contains answers

to every human need, and praying His Word
actualizes those answers in our lives by faith.

The following section of this book shows
how those answers are brought into being as a
result of praying the promises. The promise-prayers
are topically arranged, with teaching from the
Word pointing us to God's answers concerning
each topic. With each topic we've also included a
prayer that personalizes God's promises in vital,
powerful ways.

Use these prayers to meditate upon God's
Word and study His ways. Let the prayers build
faith in your heart to appropriate all God has for
you. May each prayer become a stepping-stone to
vastly new spiritual discoveries in your life.
Learning to pray this way promises to change
your life in radical ways. All God's blessings will
come to you as you enter into this exciting way to
pray.

PART 2

$\blacklozenge$

PROMISE - PRAYERS

1. Abiding in Christ

Key Promise: *"If ye abide in me, and my words abide in you, ye shall ask what ye will, and it shall be done unto you"* (John 15:7).

Abiding entails waiting, persevering, enduring, withstanding, bearing patiently, and staying fixed. To abide in Christ, therefore, is to remain in Him and to patiently wait on Him. Abiding in Him is the best of all places to be.

Andrew Murray explains, "What sacred associations are connected with that word abiding! Abiding in Christ and in His love (John 15); abiding in the Son and in the Father (1 John 2:24-28); God and Christ, the truth and the anointing abiding in us (1 John 2:14-27; 3:24). The main thought is permanent, steadfast, and immovable continuance in the place and the blessing secured to us in Christ and God. The great secret of the world is its transitoriness — it passes away with all its glory. And all who are of it partake of its vanity and uncertainty. And just as far as the Christian breathes its spirit and allows its love a place in his heart, he loses the power of abiding."

Abiding in Christ is a foundational key to answered prayer.

Promise-Prayer of Abiding

Heavenly Father, thank you for grafting me into the Living Vine — Jesus Christ, my Lord.[1] With your help, and through your grace, I will abide in Him.[2] Lord, I want to abide in Jesus and to let His words abide in me, because I know this will make me a fruitful believer.[3] Help me to so abide.

Thank you for choosing me to bear lasting fruit.[4] I know that the things I ask for in prayer, Father, will be accomplished as I abide in Christ.[5] As an abiding, fruitful Christian, I know that I will not be ashamed when Jesus returns. When He reappears I will have the confidence that comes from abiding in Christ.[6] This knowledge causes me to rejoice in you.

Help me to delight myself in your statutes, Father, so that I will never forget your Word.[7] Through your grace, I will let your Word dwell richly within me.[8] Your Word is a lamp unto my feet, and a light unto my path.[9] It's wonderful to know that abiding in Christ, and letting His Word abide in me will keep me from sin.[10] Thank you, Lord.

Throughout my life, with your help, I will abide in Christ and walk in Him and His Word.[11] Even now, as I draw near to you, Father, I know you are drawing near to me.[12]

References: *(1) John 15:1; (2) John 15:4; (3) John 15:8; (4) John 15:16; (5) John 15:7; (6) 1 John 2:28; (7) Psalms 119:16; (8) Colossians 3:16; (9) Psalms 119:105; (10) 1 John 3:6; (11) John 15:7; (12) James 4:8.*

2. Abundant Living

Key Promise: *"I have come that they may have life, and that they may have it more abundantly"* (John 10:10, NKJV).

Abundance is the state of having great plenty, ample supplies, and more than enough. This is what Jesus promises to us. He said, "But seek ye first the kingdom of God, and His righteousness; and all these things shall be added unto you" (Matt. 6:33). He promises to meet all our needs and to give us abundance if we will let Him be the Lord of our lives. When Jesus is truly Lord, we walk in righteousness each step of the way.

There are several kinds of abundance that we enjoy as promise-believers. First and foremost, there is spiritual abundance: "Blessed be the God and Father of our Lord Jesus Christ, who has blessed us with every spiritual blessing in the heavenly places in Christ" (Eph. 1:3, NKJV).

Next, there is physical-health abundance: "But if the Spirit of Him who raised Jesus from the dead dwells in you, He who raised Christ from the dead will also give life to your mortal bodies through His Spirit who dwells in you" (Rom. 8:11, NKJV).

Finally, there is material abundance: "Beloved, I wish above all things that thou mayest prosper and be in health, even as thy soul prospereth" (3 John 2).

Promise-Prayer of Abundance

Lord God, I thank you that you will make me plenteous in goods and health.[1] I know you are making me the head, and not the tail, and I will always be able to live above the circumstances of life, not beneath them if I will do your commandments.[2] Help me to do your commandments at all times, Father.

Your promise of abundance is truly over-whelming to me. Thank you for rebuking the devourer for my sake, Master.[3] I shall remember you always, and through your grace, I will put you first in my life at all times.[4] I know, Lord, that it is you who gives me the power to enjoy abundance in every area of my life.[5] Thank you, Father.

I want to obey you, Lord. You are my Shepherd, and because you are, I know I shall never experience want.[6] As I hearken to your voice, so many blessings overtake me. I am blessed in the city and in the field. The fruit of my body and the fruit of my ground are blessed, and so are my baskets and my storehouses of supplies. You bless me, Lord, as I come in and as I go out, and you cause my enemies to be smitten before me. As they come against me in one way, you cause them to flee before me in seven ways.[7] Thank you for the abundant promises of your Word, Father.

References: *(1) Deuteronomy 28:11; (2) Deuteronomy 28:13; (3) Malachi 3:11; (4) Matthew 6:33; (5) Luke 6:38; (6) Psalms 23:1; (7) Deuteronomy 28:2-7.*

3. Access to God

Key Promise: *"For through him we both have access by one Spirit unto the Father" (Eph. 2:18).*

God speaks to us through His Word, and He asks us to speak to Him through prayer. Prayer gives us access to our heavenly Father who knows what we need even before we express that need to Him. Jesus said, "Your Father knows the things you have need of before you ask Him" (Matt. 6:8, NKJV).

R.A. Torrey writes, "Prayers are hindered by unbelief. God demands that we believe His Word absolutely. To question it is to make Him a liar. Many of us do that when we plead His promises. Is it any wonder that our prayers are not answered? How many prayers are hindered by our wretched unbelief! We go to God and ask Him for something that is positively promised in His Word, and then we only half expect to get it. 'Let not that man think that he shall receive any thing of the Lord.'"

The promises of God give us access to the very heart of God where His desires for all His children are born. His Word shows us that He wants to bless us, and one of the greatest blessings of all is the direct-line fellowship we have with Him. "For there is one God and one Mediator between God and men, the Man Christ Jesus" (1 Tim. 2:5, NKJV). Through the name and blood of Jesus we have access to the Holy of Holies, the throne-room of Almighty God himself.

Promise-Prayer of Access

Throughout this day, I will obey you by rejoicing always, and I will pray without ceasing. Lord God, I give thanks to you in everything, because I know this is your will for me.[1] As I draw near to you, I know you are drawing near to me.[2] Thank you, Lord. I pray to you in faith, nothing wavering, because I know that he who wavers is like a wave of the sea that is driven and tossed by the wind.[3] Help me to be consistent in my Christian walk.

I claim the beautiful promises of your Word minute by minute and step by step as I go along my way. As you lead me, Father, I will pray always with all prayer and supplication.[4] I delight to give myself continually to prayer and to your Word.[5] As I pray to you, Lord, I do so with confidence, knowing that Jesus is interceding for me and with me as I pray.[6] Thank you, Father.

As I pray in Jesus' name I am blessed with joy and I know I will receive answers to all my prayers.[7] In your presence, Lord, I will constantly abide, because I know that there is fullness of joy in your presence.[8] Thank you for giving me access to your presence through prayer and for giving fullness of joy to me.

References: (1) 1 Thessalonians 5:16-18; (2) James 4:8; (3) James 1:6; (4) Ephesians 6:18; (5) Acts 6:2-4; (6) Hebrews 4:14-15; (7) John 16:24; (8) Psalms 16:11.

4. Adoration of God

Key Promise: *"Blessed be God, even the Father of our Lord Jesus Christ, the Father of mercies, and the God of all comfort" (2 Cor. 1:3).*

Jesus said, "But the hour cometh, and now is, when the true worshippers shall worship the Father in spirit and in truth: for the Father seeketh such to worship him. God is a Spirit: and they that worship him must worship him in spirit and in truth" (John 4:22-23). Adoration is a chief component of true spiritual worship. In fact, it literally means to worship or to honor someone or something. When we are adoring God, therefore, we are worshiping, honoring, and revering Him.

To adore God is to behold Him as He is — ". . . the Father of lights, with whom is no variableness, neither shadow of turning" (James 1:17). As we learn to pray God's promises, we learn to adore the Lord for who He is. We adore His beauty, His glory, His wisdom, His radiance, His love, His light, His righteousness, His peace, and His Kingship. Through this process of adoration we are drawn closer to Him.

The Psalmist declares, "Know ye that the Lord he is God: it is he that hath made us, and not we ourselves; we are his people, and the sheep of his pasture" (Ps. 100:3). It is this truth that enables us to "Enter into his gates with thanksgiving, and into his courts with praise" (Ps. 100:4). This leads us to ". . . be thankful unto him, and bless his name" (Ps. 100:4).

Promise-Prayer of Adoration

Heavenly Father, I worship and adore you because you are great and you are greatly to be praised.[1] You are my God forever, and you will be my Guide even unto death.[2] You are worthy, O Lord, to receive glory, honor, adoration, and power, because you have created all things, and you created all things for your pleasure.[3] It is amazing to me, Lord, to think that you created even me for your pleasure; therefore, I want to please you in all things.

You truly are the King of kings, and the Lord of lords,[4] and I will honor, adore, and serve you throughout my life. O God, my heart is fixed. I will sing and give praise to you.[5] I will praise you, O Lord, among the people, and I will sing praises unto you among the nations, because your mercy is great above the heavens and your truth reaches to the clouds. Be exalted, O God, above the heavens, and let your glory shine above all the earth.[6]

Dear God, you are my refuge and my strength, a very present help to me in times of trouble. Therefore, I will not fear.[7] As I adore you, Father, I will be still and know that you are my God. You will be exalted among the heathen, and throughout the earth.[8]

References: (1) Psalms 48:1; (2) Psalms 48:14; (3) Revelation 4:11; (4) Revelation 19:16; (5) Psalms 108:1; (6) Psalms 108:1-5; (7) Psalms 46:1-2; (8) Psalms 46:10.

5. Amazing Grace

Key Promise: *"For by grace are ye saved through faith; and that not of yourselves: it is the gift of God: Not of works, lest any man should boast" (Eph. 2:8-9).*

God's grace is greater than all our sin. The Bible says, "For the Lord God is a sun and shield: the Lord will give grace and glory: no good thing will he withhold from them that walk uprightly" (Ps. 84:11). Now that's grace — God will give good things to us.

It all begins when we receive Jesus Christ as our Lord and Savior. The Apostle Paul wrote, "By grace are ye saved through faith; and that not of yourselves: it is the gift of God: Not of works, lest any man should boast" (Eph. 2:8-9). This is the biblical definition of grace: a gift of God that is received through faith, not as a direct result of good works.

God's grace involves His favor, as the writer of the Book of Proverbs points out: "For whoso findeth me findeth life, and shall obtain favour of the Lord" (Prov. 8:35). This is a direct promise of grace from God, and we can claim it and pray it as His children, remembering that God always keeps His promises.

The Psalmist concurs with this promise. Under the inspiration of God he wrote, "For thou, Lord, wilt bless the righteous; with favour wilt thou compass him as with a shield" (Ps. 5:12). The amazing grace of God is always at work in our lives.

Promise-Prayer of Amazing Grace

I come boldly to your throne of grace, Father, because I know you will give me your mercy and grace in all my times of need.[1] I thank you, Lord, for your promise that you will bless the righteous with your favor which is encompassing my life like a shield.[2] Your Grace imparts righteousness to me.[3] Thank you for granting life and favor to me, Lord, and for your visitation which has preserved my spirit.[4] I love you, Father.

You are so wonderful, Lord, and I love you with all my heart. Your amazing grace has made me accepted in the fellowship of your beloved.[5] Hallelujah! Thank you for the promise that all things are for the sake of believers so that your abundant grace might, through the thanksgiving of many, redound to your glory.[6] You have made me very thankful, Lord.

I am totally dependent on your grace, Father. In finding you, I found life, and I recognize the fact that you have showered your favor upon me.[7] You are blessing me, and you will always bless me, because I hold you in reverential fear, Father.[8] As you gave great power to your apostles who witnessed the Resurrection of Jesus Christ, I know you will continue to give your amazing grace to me.[9]

References: (1) Hebrews 4:16; (2) Psalms 5:12; (3) 1 Corinthians 1:30; (4) Job 10:12; (5) Ephesians 1:6; (6) 2 Corinthians 4:15; (7) Proverbs 8:35; (8) Psalms 115:13; (9) Acts 4:33.

6. Answered Prayer

Key Promise: *"If we know that he hear us, whatsoever we ask, we know that we have the petitions that we desired of him"* (1 John 5:15).

The Prophet Jeremiah gave us a wonderful prayer promise when he wrote, under the inspiration of the Holy Spirit, "Call unto me, and I will answer thee, and shew thee great and mighty things, which thou knowest not" (Jer. 33:3).

Reuben Archer Torrey wrote, "Our whole life should be a life of prayer. We should walk in constant communion with God. There should be a constant looking upward to God. We should walk so habitually in His presence that even when we awake in the night it would be the most natural thing for us to speak to Him in thanksgiving or petition." This admonition is similar to what Paul wrote: "Rejoice evermore. Pray without ceasing. In every thing give thanks: for this is the will of God in Christ Jesus concerning you" (1 Thess. 5:16-18).

It is clear that God wants us to pray. Prayer is an amazing source of power in our lives. As we learn to pray according to the will of God (as it is revealed in His Word), we will find answers to our prayers. The Apostle John points out: "And this is the confidence that we have in him, that, if we ask any thing according to his will, he heareth us: And if we know that he hear us, whatsoever we ask, we know that we have the petitions that we desired of him" (1 John 5:14-15).

What a wonderful prayer promise this is!

Promise-Prayer of Answered Prayer

Thank you, Father, for your wonderful promise that you will answer me even before I call unto you, and while I am yet speaking, you will hear me.[1] It is so reassuring to know that you know what I need even before I express it unto you.[2] As I ask, I know it will be given to me. As I knock, I know it will be opened unto me. As I seek, I know I shall find. Your promise tells me, Lord, that everyone who asks receives, and he who seeks finds, and he who knocks is welcomed by an open door.[3] Thank you, Lord.

When I pray in faith, Father, your Word promises me that I will receive what I ask for.[4] The promises of your Word give me the faith to believe that whatever I ask for in prayer, believing, you will give to me.[5]

You do hear my cries.[6] I will keep on abiding in you, because your Word promises me that if I abide in you, and let your Word abide in me, I shall ask what I will and it shall be granted.[7] Without you, Lord, I can do nothing.[8]

References: (1) Isaiah 65:24; (2) Matthew 6:8; (3) Matthew 7:7-8; (4) Mark 11:24; (5) Matthew 21:22; (6) Psalms 145:18-19; (7) John 15:7; (8) John 15:5.

7. Atonement

Key Promise: *"In whom we have redemption through his blood, the forgiveness of sins, according to the riches of his grace"* (Eph. 1:7).

Jesus Christ, the Lamb of God, atoned for our sins when He died on the cross. This atonement made reconciliation between God and mankind possible. Someone said, "Atonement is at-one-ment with God." Through Jesus' atoning work on the cross we are able to be "at one" with God, our heavenly Father.

Paul wrote, "For if, when we were enemies, we were reconciled to God by the death of his Son, much more, being reconciled, we shall be saved by his life. And not only so, but we also joy in God through our Lord Jesus Christ, by whom we have now received the atonement" (Rom. 5:10-11).

Indeed, we have great reason for joy, because ". . . now in Christ Jesus ye who sometimes were far off are made nigh by the blood of Christ. For he is our peace, who hath made both one, and hath broken down the middle wall of partition between us" (Eph. 2:13-14).

The Atonement is a cause for genuine celebration. It gives us direct access to our Father in heaven. "For there is one God, and one mediator between God and men, the man Christ Jesus; Who gave himself a ransom for all, to be testified in due time" (1 Tim. 2:5-6).

Promise-Prayer of Atonement

Lord God, thank you so much that you sent your only begotten Son to become the sacrifice for my sins.[1] For me, He suffered from the foundation of the world, but through His suffering, He has put away sin once and for all.[2] I am so thankful that Jesus offered himself to bear the sins of many. Because of this, I know that He will appear the second time without sin, unto salvation.[3] My heart fills with praise to you, Father.

As I look back upon my life, Lord, I realize how deeply sinful I used to be, and how far I fell short of your glory. Through your grace, provided by the blood of Jesus Christ, I was justified freely and I was gloriously redeemed. Thank you for sending Jesus to be the atoning sacrifice for me. By faith in the blood of Jesus Christ I accept the remission of my sins.[4] Thank you, Father.

While I was yet a sinner, you commended your love to me, Lord. Christ died for me, and He set me free from my sins.[5] Now I know that I have received your gift of eternal life through Jesus Christ, my Lord.[6] Thank you, Father.

References: *(1) John 3:16; (2) Hebrews 9:26; (3) Hebrews 9:28; (4) Romans 3:25; (5) Romans 5:8; (6) Romans 6:23.*

8. Attitudes

Key Promise: *"He hath shewed thee, O man, what is good; and what doth the Lord require of thee, but to do justly, and to love mercy, and to walk humbly with thy God"* (Mic. 6:8).

The Word of God commands, "Keep thy heart with all diligence; for out of it are the issues of life" (Prov. 4:23). It is so important for us to keep the attitudes of our hearts in complete congruence with the Word of God. As we learn to focus on the promises of God instead of the problems of life, the attitudes of our hearts begin to line up with all God wants and has for us.

The fruit of the Spirit, as outlined in Galatians 5:22-23, reveal what our heart-attitudes should be: "But the fruit of the Spirit is love, joy, peace, longsuffering, gentleness, goodness, faith, meekness, temperance: against such there is no law." Every day we should ask God to help us to produce the fruit of the Spirit in all the relationships and responsibilities of our lives.

As fruit-bearing Christians, therefore, we go forth into the world with the right attitudes. We learn how to "Let all bitterness, and wrath, and anger, and clamour, and evil speaking, be put away from you, with all malice; And be ye kind one to another, tenderhearted, forgiving one another, even as God for Christ's sake hath forgiven you" (Eph. 4:31-32).

Promise-Prayer for Right Attitudes

Lord, I want to keep the attitudes of my heart right at all times. Therefore, I ask you to help me to walk in love as Jesus did.[1] Help me to do justly, love mercy, and walk humbly with you.[2] With your help, Father, I will let the same attitude of mind be in me that was in Christ Jesus. Like Him, I want to be obedient to your will.[3]

As you work within me both to will and to work for your good pleasure,[4] Father, I pray that the fruit of your Spirit will be produced in my life.[5]

Help me to walk in your Spirit, Lord, so that I will have the right attitudes at all times.[6]

Thank you for your Word which is a lamp unto my path and a light unto my feet.[7] It shows me how I am to live and it shows me clearly what the attitudes of my heart should be. I will walk in the light of your Word, Father, for the rest of my days, and I know this will bring the necessary changes to the attitudes of my heart.

References: (1) Ephesians 5:2; (2) Micah 6:8; (3) Philippians 2:5-8; (4) Philippians 2:13; (5) Galatians 5:22-23; (6) Galatians 5:16; (7) Psalms 119:105.

9. Belief

Key Promise: *"With men it is impossible, but not with God: for with God all things are possible" (Mark 10:27).*

Belief is the trustful confidence that comes to us through faith. It is the correct attitude and state of being for every Christian. The writer of the Book of Hebrews points out, "Without faith it is impossible to please Him, for he who comes to God must believe that He is, and that He is a rewarder of those who diligently seek Him" (Heb. 11:6, NKJV).

What you believe determines how you will live, what you will say, and how you will pray. If you believe the promises of God, you will naturally incorporate them into your prayer life and hope will rise in your heart. If you believe the promises of God, you will live, think, and act accordingly. It's all a matter of focus.

To believe God's promises we must believe His Word, and as Paul points out, "Faith cometh by hearing, and hearing by the word of God" (Rom. 10:17). It is clear, therefore, that if we want to have faith, we must dive into the Word of God and extract all of its promises and apply them to our lives and prayers.

Believe, believe, believe. Then you will receive, receive, receive.

Promise-Prayer of Belief

Heavenly Father, my heart's desire is to walk by faith, not by sight, at all times.[1] I will immerse myself in your Word so that my faith will grow.[2] With your help, I will keep looking unto Jesus who is the Author and Finisher of my faith.[3] As I pray, I will believe that I will receive my requests, because your Word promises me, "What things soever ye desire, when ye pray, believe that ye receive them, and ye shall have them."[4]

You have justified me, Father, therefore, I will live by faith.[5] Even though I have never seen you, Lord, I love you. Even though I have never seen you, I believe in you with all my heart. The belief you've imparted to me gives me an unspeakable joy that is full of your radiant glory.[6] The faith your Word imparts to me makes me victorious in every area of my life.[7] Thank you, Lord.

I know that you give to me according to my faith, Father.[8] Therefore, I will believe that all things are possible with you.[9] Lord, thank you for enabling me to be a true believer at all times.

References: *(1) 2 Corinthians 5:7; (2) Romans 10:17; (3) Hebrews 12:2; (4) Mark 11:24; (5) Romans 1:17; (6) 1 Peter 1:7-8; (7) 1 John 5:4; (8) Matthew 9:29; (9) Mark 9:23.*

10. Blessing

Key Promise: *"Blessed is the man that feareth the Lord, that delighteth greatly in his commandments. His seed shall be mighty upon earth: the generation of the upright shall be blessed. Wealth and riches shall be in his house: and his righteousness endureth for ever"* *(Ps. 112:1-3).*

When she was eight years old, Fanny Crosby wrote a poem that expressed her faith: "O, what a happy soul am I, though blind and cannot see. I am resolved that in this world, contented I will be." Her hymns, such as "Blessed Assurance," show that she held onto her resolve throughout the years.

Even though she was blind, Fanny Crosby knew and enjoyed the blessings of God. She believed that God was out to bless her, and she prayed, preached, and sang accordingly.

God wants to bless you. He is a God of blessing. The reality is that He has already blessed us with every spiritual blessing in Christ Jesus. Paul wrote, "Blessed be the God and Father of our Lord Jesus Christ, who has blessed us with every spiritual blessing in the heavenly places in Christ" (Eph. 1:3, NKJV). We already have all the spiritual blessings we need — the Bible, prayer, fellowship, worship, praise, faith, hope, and love. We are blessed!

God is able to do ". . . exceedingly abundantly above all that we ask or think" (Eph. 3:20, NKJV). Now that is blessing!

Promise-Prayer of Blessing

Thank you,[1] Father, for blessing me with every spiritual[2] and temporal[3] blessing. I am truly blessed. You love me, Father, and I love you.[4]

Lord, you have redeemed me from the hand of the enemy.[5] The blood of Christ has set me free.[6] My sins have been forgiven.[7]

You have given me so much, including the spirit of wisdom and revelation that enables me to know you and your ways more fully.[8] You have given me enlightenment that helps me to see and know the hope to which you have called me.[9]

Thank you, Father, for giving me your blessing in every part of my life. Your blessing brings me prosperity,[10] health,[11] victory,[12] and joy.[13] I truly am blessed, Father, and I praise you for all the blessings you have given so freely to me.[14]

Make me a blessing to others by helping me to be kind, tender-hearted, and forgiving even as you for Christ's sake have forgiven me.[15]

References: *(1) Philippians 4:6; (2) Ephesians 1:3; (3) Philippians 4:19; (4) 1 John 4:19; (5) Psalms 107:2; (6) 1 John 1:7; (7) 1 John 1:9; (8) Ephesians 1:18; (9) Ephesians 4:4; (10) Psalms 1:3; (11) 3 John 2; (12) Isaiah 25:8; (13) Romans 15:13; (14) Psalms 129:8; (15) Ephesians 4:32.*

11. Blood of Jesus

Key Promise: *"In whom we have redemption through his blood, the forgiveness of sins, according to the riches of his grace"* (Eph. 1:7).

Andrew Murray wrote, ". . . Christians can never know too much about the truths the blood proclaims. There can be no freedom of approach to God, nor fellowship with Him, apart from a truly vital and powerful experience of the blood of Christ. Its power is a hidden, spiritual, divine reality, and therefore can be experienced only in a heart thus humbly and entirely submitted to the Spirit of God."

The Apostle John shows us how the blood of Jesus and the Holy Spirit work together to unleash great power in our lives: "There are three that bear witness in earth, the Spirit, and the water, and the blood: and these agree in one" (1 John 5:8). He also wrote, "But if we walk in the light, as he is in the light, we have fellowship one with another, and the blood of Jesus Christ his Son cleanseth us from all sin" (1 John 1:7).

It is Jesus' blood that gives us access to God, as Paul pointed out, "But now in Christ Jesus ye who sometimes were far off are made nigh by the blood of Christ" (Eph. 2:13). The blood gives power to our prayer lives, our testimonies, our faith, and our daily walk. As we claim God's promises about the blood of Jesus through prayer, amazing and miraculous things begin to happen.

Promise-Prayer Exalting the Blood of Jesus

Father, thank you for Jesus Christ who shed His blood on Calvary's cross for me.[1] He has justified me through His blood so that I know I shall be saved from wrath through Him.[2]

As I read the promises of your Word, Lord, faith rises in my heart to receive and appropriate all that the blood of Jesus affords to me. I will declare His righteousness, and I will praise you for your forbearance that enabled the blood to wipe away my sins. Father, you have made it possible for me to be justified through faith in Christ.[3] Thank you, Lord.

I believe your Word, and I desire to walk in the light of your Word as Christ is in the light so that I will have meaningful fellowship with you and with other believers. The blood of your Son, Jesus Christ, cleanses me from all my sins.[4] His blood purges my conscience of dead works and it enables me to serve you, loving Father.[5]

It is so wonderful to realize that I was not redeemed with corruptible things, such as silver and gold, but I was redeemed (bought back from sin and Satan) by the blood of Christ who is my Savior and Lord. His blood enables me to believe in you, Father. All my faith and hope are in you.[6]

References: (1) Romans 5:8; (2) Romans 5:9;
(3) Romans 3:24-26; (4) 1 John 1:7; (5) Hebrews 9:14;
(6) 1 Peter 1:18-21.

12. Boldness

Key Promise: *"Let us draw near with a true heart in full assurance of faith, having our hearts sprinkled from an evil conscience, and our bodies washed with pure water" (Heb. 10:22).*

If God's "exceeding great and precious promises" provide us with all the blessings Peter outlines (see 2 Pet. 1:4-8), we have reason to be the most confident people in the world. Confidence in God and His promises makes us bold in faith.

"Let us hold fast the profession of our faith without wavering; (for he is faithful that promised;)" (Heb. 10:23). "Cast not away therefore your confidence, which hath great recompense of reward. For ye have need of patience, that, after ye have done the will of God, ye might receive the promise. For yet a little while, and he that shall come will come, and will not tarry" (Heb. 10:35-37). Boldness comes from knowing that God is always faithful to us.

God always keeps His promises. We can count on His Word. If He said it, we can truly believe it. We can stand upon His promises without wavering, and as we do, we find confidence and boldness rising within us, and we realize, "Now this is the confidence that we have in Him, that if we ask anything according to His will, He hears us" (1 John 5:14, NKJV).

Promise-Prayer of Boldness

This is the confidence that I have in you, Father: if I ask anything according to your will (as it is revealed to me in your Word) I know you will hear me. And I know that because you hear me, no matter what I ask (as long as it agrees with your will/your Word), will be granted to me.[1] Thank you, Father.

Therefore, I come boldly before your throne, Lord, knowing that I will obtain your mercy and grace whenever I have a need.[2] The promises of your Word impart great faith and boldness to my spirit, Father, and because of them I will not be slothful. They enable me to be a follower of those, who through faith and patience, inherit your promises.[3]

You are my strength and boldness, Lord. You make my feet like the feet of a deer. You enable me to walk in high places.[4] I believe in Jesus Christ, and I know that this will enable me to accomplish great things in His name.

The boldness you impart to me empowers me to realize that I can do all things through Christ who strengthens me.[5] You are my helper, and I will never fear what others can do to me.[6] I am confident that you have begun a good work in me, and you will complete your work in me.[7]

References: (1) 1 John 5:14-15; (2) Hebrews 4:16; (3) Hebrews 6:12; (4) Habakkuk 3:19; (5) Philippians 4:13; (6) Hebrews 13:6; (7) Philippians 1:6.

13. Brokenness

Key Promise: *"The sacrifices of God are a broken spirit: a broken and a contrite heart, O God, thou wilt not despise" (Ps. 51:17).*

There is no doubt about it — we need the Lord. An anonymous writer expressed his concept of brokenness before God this way: "Fear not, you are inadequate." It is the erroneous belief that we have to be perfect before we can be accepted by God that leads so many people into failure. Most fear comes from the idea that we have to be perfectly adequate in whatever we do. Brokenness before God leads us to understand that everything we are and have is the direct result of His workmanship in our lives. This is a wonderful and peaceful realization.

The Bible says, "Pride goeth before destruction, and an haughty spirit before a fall. Better it is to be of an humble spirit with the lowly, than to divide the spoil with the proud" (Prov. 16:18-19). The opposite of pride is humility, and humility is the attitude of heart that comes when we fully recognize our brokenness before God.

"But he giveth more grace. Wherefore he saith, God resisteth the proud, but giveth grace unto the humble. Submit yourselves therefore to God. Resist the devil, and he will flee from you . . . . Humble yourselves in the sight of the Lord, and he shall lift you up" (James 4:6-7, 10).

Promise-Prayer of Brokenness

Have mercy upon me, O God, according to your lovingkindness.[1] Let my heart be broken with the things that break your heart. Change my heart, Lord, and make me more like you. I know you desire truth in my inner self. As I humble myself before you, Lord, make me to know wisdom in my inmost heart.[2]

Hide your face from my sins, and blot out all my iniquities.[3] Create in me a clean heart, O God, and renew a steadfast spirit within me.[4] Restore to me the joy of your salvation, and uphold me by your generous Spirit so that I will be able to teach transgressors your ways, and so that sinners will be converted to you.[5]

Thank you for your promise that you will be near to those that are of a broken heart. You save those who have a contrite spirit. Though the afflictions of the righteous may be many, you, Lord, will deliver me from them all.[6] Lord, I know that without you I can do nothing,[7] but through you I can do all things, because you strengthen me.[8] Therefore, I humble myself before your greatness, and I totally submit my life to you. As I draw near to you, I know you are drawing near to me.[9] Thank you, Father.

References: *(1) Psalms 51:1; (2) Psalms 51:6; (3) Psalms 51:9; (4) Psalms 51:10; (5) Psalms 51:12-13; (6) Psalms 34:18-19; (7) John 15:5; (8) Philippians 4:13; (9) James 4:6-8.*

14. Calling

Key Promise: *"For the gifts and calling of God are without repentance" (Rom. 11:29).*

Each one of us has been called. In fact, we are the *ecclesia* — the called-out ones. God has called us out of the kingdom of the world, and He has translated us into His glorious kingdom. (See Col. 1:13.) Jesus said, "You did not choose Me, but I chose you and appointed you that you should go and bear fruit, and that your fruit should remain, that whatever you ask the Father in My name He may give you" (John 15:16, NKJV).

We have been called or chosen to be fruitful Christians. God promises that our fruit will remain, and He promises to answer our prayers. We will bear lasting fruit for Him, and whatever we ask the Father for, in the name of Jesus, will be granted to us.

A wonderful Bible promise comes to mind when we become fully aware of God's calling on our lives. It is found in Paul's Epistle to the Romans: "And we know that all things work together for good to those who love God, to those who are the called according to His purpose" (Rom. 8:28, NKJV). We have been called to fulfill God's purpose for our lives, and when we truly understand this, we can rest confident in the certainty that everything is working together for good in our lives.

Promise-Prayer in Response to God's Calling

Blessed be my God and Father, the Father of my Lord and Savior, Jesus Christ, who has blessed me with every spiritual blessing in the heavenly places in Christ.[1] You chose me in Christ before the foundation of the world so that I would become holy and without blame before Him in love. Thank you for predestining me to be adopted into your family, Lord. It thrills me to know that I am now your child.[2]

Give me the grace to obey you in all things, Father. Jesus tells me, "You are My friends if you do whatever I command you."[3] He has given me His personal Emancipation Proclamation: "No longer do I call you servants, for a servant does not know what his master is doing; but I have called you friends, for all things that I heard from My Father I have made known to you."[4] Thank you for calling me out of the world, Father.[5]

With your help, Lord, I will make every effort to make my calling and election sure.[6] I will walk in a manner that is worthy of my high calling,[7] and I will forget those things that are behind me as I reach forward to those things which are ahead. I will keep on pressing on toward the goal for the prize of your high calling in Christ Jesus.[8]

References: (1) Ephesians 1:3; (2) Ephesians 1:5; (3) John 15:14; (4) John 15:15; (5) John 15:19; (6) 2 Peter 1:10; (7) Ephesians 4:1; (8) Philippians 3:13-14.

15. Comfort

Key Promise: *"If ye love me, keep my commandments, and I will pray the Father, and he shall give you another Comforter, that he may abide with you for ever" (John 14:15-16).*

The Word says, "For the Lord hath comforted his people, and will have mercy upon his afflicted" (Isa. 49:13). In truth, our God is ". . . the Father of mercies, and the God of all comfort; Who comforteth us in all our tribulation, that we may be able to comfort them which are in any trouble, by the comfort wherewith we ourselves are comforted of God" (2 Cor. 1:3-4). This verse shows us that comfort is not a selfish thing; it is given to us so that we can share it with others.

God promises to give us: ". . . beauty for ashes, the oil of joy for mourning, the garment of praise for the spirit of heaviness" so that we will be ". . . called trees of righteousness, the planting of the Lord, that he might be glorified" (Isa. 61:3).

The comfort God gives, therefore, does not necessarily make us comfortable, but it does meet our need in times of loss and discouragement. He promises to give us His comfort. In fact, the Holy Spirit is the divine Comforter as Jesus pointed out, "But the Comforter, which is the Holy Ghost, whom the Father will send in my name, he shall teach you all things, and bring all things to your remembrance, whatsoever I have said unto you" (John 14:26).

Promise-Prayer of Comfort

Dear Lord, help me to experience your comforting presence in my life, and always to comfort others with the same comfort you've given to me.[1] Help me to walk in your anointing which will enable me to preach good tidings unto the meek, to bind up the broken-hearted, to proclaim liberty to the captives and the opening of prisons to them that are bound, to proclaim your acceptable year and your day of vengeance.

Thank you for your Comforter, the Holy Spirit,[2] who comforts me when I mourn and gives me beauty for ashes and the oil of joy for mourning. Because of your comfort, Lord, I will wear the garment of praise instead of the spirit of heaviness, and I will be called a tree of righteousness, and I will glorify your name.[3]

Father, I know you love me and you have given me your everlasting consolation and good hope through grace. This brings great comfort to my heart and it establishes me in every good word and work.[4] Thank you, Father.

I know you will always comfort me in times of loss and mourning.[5] Your Word always brings life and comfort to me in times of affliction, Lord.[6] Thank you for your comforting presence in my life.

References: *(1) 2 Corinthians 1:4; (2) John 14:26; (3) Isaiah 61:1-3; (4) 2 Thessalonians 2:16-17; (5) Matthew 5:4; (6) Psalms 119:50.*

16. Commitment

Key Promise: *"Nevertheless I am not ashamed: for I know whom I have believed, and am persuaded that he is able to keep that which I have committed unto him against that day"* (2 Tim. 1:12).

Oswald Chambers wrote, "The great word of Jesus to His disciples is 'abandon.'" To commit our lives to Christ is to be totally abandoned to Him. It is absolute surrender.

Billy Graham reveals the implications of commitment to us: "Yielding to Christ is confessing every known sin in your life, yielding every area of your life. It means yielding your girl friend, your boy friend, your family, your business, your career, your ambitions, your soul, the innermost thoughts and depths of your heart; yielding them all to Christ, holding nothing back."

So commitment is abandonment, surrender, and yielding, and it is so much more. Jesus tells us, "Whosoever therefore shall confess me before men, him will I confess also before my Father which is in heaven . . . . And he that taketh not his cross, and followeth after me is not worthy of me. He that findeth his life shall lose it: and he that loseth his life for my sake shall find it" (Matt. 10:32, 38-39).

Oswald Chambers takes it a step further when he writes, "You cannot consecrate what is not yours. There is only one thing you can consecrate to God, and that is the right to yourself."

Promise-Prayer of Commitment

Loving Lord, I commit my life to you. I confess with my mouth that Jesus is Lord, and I believe in my heart that you have raised Him from the dead. Thank you for saving me. With my heart I believe unto righteousness, and with my mouth I make my confession unto salvation, and because I believe in Christ, I know you will never let me be ashamed.[1] Thank you, Lord.

I trust completely in you, Lord. With your help, I will do good. I will delight myself in you, and I know you will give me the desires of my heart. As I commit my way to you and trust in you, I know you will bless me, and you will bring forth my righteousness as the light. The realization of these wonderful promises enables me to rest in you, Lord, and to wait patiently for you. Therefore, I will not worry.[2]

Father, I express my faith to you. I want to please you. I know that all those who come to you must believe fully and unreservedly in you. I know you are a Rewarder of all those who diligently seek you.[3] I will seek you, Lord, while you may be found, and I will call upon you when you are near.[4] I will draw near to you, and I know you will draw near to me.[5]

References: (1) Romans 10:9-11; (2) Psalms 37:3-7; (3) Hebrews 11:6; (4) Isaiah 55:6; (5) James 4:8.

17. Compassion

Key Promise: *"But thou, O Lord, art a God full of compassion, and gracious, longsuffering, and plenteous in mercy and truth"* (Ps. 86:15).

Compassion is a quality of life that enables us to feel what others feel and to enter into their experience. It is empathy of the highest kind. Jesus has compassion on each of us. When He saw the multitudes, in all their pain and neediness, ". . . He was moved with compassion for them, because they were weary and scattered, like sheep having no shepherd" (Matt. 9:36, NKJV).

As our High Priest, seated at God's right hand in the heavenly kingdom, Jesus continues to be moved with compassion in our behalf: "Seeing then that we have a great High Priest who has passed through the heavens, Jesus the Son of God, let us hold fast our confession. For we do not have a High Priest who cannot sympathize with our weaknesses, but was in all points tempted as we are, yet without sin" (Heb. 4:14-15, NKJV).

In learning to be compassionate, we need to become like Jesus in all things, to let His life be expressed through us. "For to this you were called, because Christ also suffered for us, leaving us an example, that you should follow His steps" (1 Pet. 2:21, NKJV).

Our responsibility is to let the compassion of Jesus flow through us to others.

Promise-Prayer of Compassion

Loving Father, help me to obey your Word which directs me to: "Execute true justice, show mercy and compassion everyone to his brother."[1] Thank you for showing me what is good, and what you require from me. With your help, Father, I will do justly, love mercy, and walk humbly with you.[2] This is my heart's desire.

I thank you, Lord, that your mercy keeps me from being consumed. Your compassions never fail. My soul declares, "You are my portion; therefore, I hope in you!" You are good to all who wait for you, to everyone who seeks you. Therefore, I hope and wait quietly for you.[3]

Help me to be like you, to follow in your steps of mercy and compassion.[4] Whenever I see someone overtaken in any kind of fault or failure, I want you to use me to help restore that person in a spirit of gentleness as I consider myself, lest I would be tempted in the same way. Help me to become a burden-bearer in the same way you are, Lord. I want to bear the burdens of others with compassion, and thereby fulfill the law of Christ, which is love.[5]

References: (1) Zechariah 7:9; (2) Micah 6:8; (3) Lamentations 3:22-25; (4) 1 Peter 2:21; (5) Galatians 6:1-2.

18. Contentment

Key Promise: *"Let your conversation be without covetousness; and be content with such things as ye have: for he hath said, I will never leave thee, nor forsake thee" (Heb. 13:5).*

Contentment implies satisfaction, rest, and peace, and the only way to find true contentment in this world is through Jesus Christ who said, "Peace I leave with you, My peace I give to you; not as the world gives do I give to you. Let not your heart be troubled, neither let it be afraid" (John 14:27, NKJV).

Some rules that govern contentment include the following: Keep your heart free from hate, your mind free from worry. Live simply. Expect little, give much. Sing often. Pray always. Forget your self. Think of others and their feelings. Fill your heart with love. Scatter sunshine wherever you go.

Two golden keys to contentment, therefore, are keeping our minds on the Lord and trusting in Him. These truths are echoed throughout the Bible. "Let us lay aside every weight, and the sin which so easily ensnares us, and let us run with endurance the race that is set before us, looking unto Jesus, the author and finisher of our faith" (Heb. 12:1-2, NKJV). In Proverbs, we read, "Trust in the Lord with all your heart, and lean not on your own understanding; in all your ways acknowledge Him, and He shall direct your paths" (Prov. 3:5-6, NKJV).

Promise-Prayer of Contentment

Lord, thank you for promising contentment to me. I will keep my mind stayed on you and I will trust you forever. Thank you for the perfect peace this brings to me.[1] I will replace all worrying with prayer and supplication and thanksgiving. I will let all my requests be made known unto you. In so doing, Lord, I receive your wonderful blessing of peace — a peace that surpasses understanding. It is the peace you have promised to me, and it keeps my heart and mind through Christ Jesus.[2]

I can do all things through my Lord and Savior.[3] Thank you, Father, for His example and for His power that enables me to be content in whatever state I find myself.[4] I hold your promises within my heart, and I know that all things work together for good in my life because I love you and you have called me according to your purpose.[5] Thank you, Father.

You guide me continually, Lord, and you always satisfy my soul, even in the dry times. You are making me like a watered garden, like a spring with unfailing waters.[6] Thank you, Father. The godliness and righteousness you have imparted to me is contentment and great gain to me, Lord.[7]

References: (1) Isaiah 26:3-4; (2) Philippians 4:6-7; (3) Philippians 4:13; (4) Philippians 4:11; (5) Romans 8:28; (6) Isaiah 58:11; (7) 1 Timothy 6:6-8.

19. Courage

Key Promise: *"Wait on the Lord: be of good courage, and he shall strengthen thine heart: wait, I say, on the Lord" (Ps. 27:14).*

The Bible admonishes us, "Be strong and of good courage, do not fear nor be afraid of them; for the Lord your God, He is the One who goes with you. He will not leave you nor forsake you" (Deut. 31:6, NKJV). The context in which this verse is found is Moses' address to the people of Israel. It was Moses' birthday; he was 120 when he spoke these words.

The patriarch knew that He would not cross over the Jordan River with his people, but He wanted to encourage them with the promises of God. He assured them that God would destroy their enemies. Then he turned to his faithful lieutenant Joshua and said, "Be strong and of good courage, for you must go with this people to the land which the Lord has sworn to their fathers to give them, and you shall cause them to inherit it. And the Lord, He is the One who goes before you. He will be with you, He will not leave you nor forsake you; do not fear nor be dismayed" (Deut. 31:7-8, NKJV).

Moses was assuring Joshua and the Israelites that the Promised Land was their rightful inheritance. Nothing would keep them from entering in. It is this same message that God wants us to hear today. All His promises are for us.

Promise-Prayer of Courage

Lord, thank you for giving me courage. I will walk in the courage you provide to me throughout this day, realizing that you are with me and that you will never leave me. These realizations keep me from fear.[1] I am more than a conqueror through Christ who loves me.[2] Thank you for the fact that nothing shall ever separate me from your love, Father.[3] Your perfect love casts out all fear in my life.[4]

With your help, Father, I will never fear again, because I know you are with me. I will not be dismayed, because you are my God. You always give me strength. You always help me, and you always uphold me with the right hand of your righteousness.[5] Thank you, Lord.

You have encouraged me through your Word, Father, and I know that no weapon that is formed against me shall ever prosper, and every tongue which rises against me in judgment you shall condemn. Thank you for making this my heritage as your servant, and for giving me your righteousness which encourages me in every respect.[6]

Thank you for the courage your Word imparts to me, Father.

References: (1) Deuteronomy 31:8; (2) Romans 8:37; (3) Romans 8:38-39; (4) 1 John 4:18; (5) Isaiah 41:10; (6) Isaiah 54:17.

20. Discernment

Key Promise: *"But the natural man receiveth not the things of the Spirit of God: for they are foolishness unto him: neither can he know them, because they are spiritually discerned. But he that is spiritual judgeth all things, yet he himself is judged of no man" (1 Cor. 2:14-15).*

Discernment involves the capacity to see and to understand with the eyes of the spirit. It is a spiritual gift.

Paul wrote, "These things we also speak, not in words which man's wisdom teaches but which the Holy Spirit teaches, comparing spiritual things with spiritual. But the natural man does not receive the things of the Spirit of God, for they are foolishness to him; nor can he know them, because they are spiritually discerned. But he who is spiritual judges all things, yet he himself is rightly judged by no one" (1 Cor. 2:13-15, NKJV).

Discernment requires a spiritual walk that is so close to God that we can sense His voice speaking to us and directing us through His Word. This results in a spiritual sensitivity that enables us to distinguish good from bad and right from wrong. Spiritual discernment is a gift that enables us to make spiritual judgments that will benefit the body of believers. Sometimes spiritual discernment is used to protect believers from "wolves in sheep's clothing." At other times it is used as a way to gain insights into the needs of others so that we may be able to minister to them and to pray more effectively for them.

Promise-Prayer for Discernment

Heavenly Father, thank you for the gift of discernment which you impart to individuals so that the Body of Christ will be edified.[1] I beseech you for greater spiritual discernment in every situation I face.

I thank you, Lord, that human eyes have not yet seen and human ears have not yet heard all the things which you have prepared for those who love you. I know this is true, and you are filling my heart with expectation.[2]

Father, reveal your deeper spiritual truths to me through your Spirit, I pray. I know that your Spirit searches all things, including the very deepest spiritual things.[3] I never want to use my carnal mind to attempt to figure things out, Lord. Instead, I want to be spiritually minded, because I know this brings me life and peace.[4]

I desire to be like Abraham, Lord, your personal friend.[5] When Jesus chose me to be His disciple He also chose me to be His friend,[6] and this fact of my faith is almost too overwhelming for me to comprehend because its implications are so far-reaching. Nonetheless, Lord, it is a privilege for me to be your friend, and I ask you to reveal to me the deep things of your Spirit.[7]

References: (1) 1 Corinthians 12:10; (2) 1 Corinthians 2:9; (3) 1 Corinthians 2:10; (4) Romans 8:6; (5) James 2:23; (6) John 15:14; (7) John 15:15.

21. Discipleship

Key Promise: *"Herein is my Father glorified, that ye bear much fruit; so shall ye be my disciples" (John 15:8).*

A disciple is one who places himself under the discipline (or teaching) of another. A disciple of Jesus Christ is a follower of Jesus and His ways.

One mark of a disciple, according to Jesus, is love. He said, "A new commandment I give to you, that you love one another; as I have loved you, that you also love one another. By this all will know that you are My disciples, if you have love for one another" (John 13:34-35, NKJV).

Another mark of a disciple, according to Jesus, is obedience. He said, "If you keep My commandments, you will abide in My love, just as I have kept My Father's commandments and abide in His love. These things I have spoken to you, that My joy may remain in you, and that your joy may be full. This is My commandment, that you love one another as I have loved you" (John 15:10-12, NKJV).

Jesus commands us to love and to obey, and He promises us that if we will practice these qualities our joy will be full. It is awe-inspiring to realize that He wants His disciples to walk in fullness of joy.

Promise-Prayer of Discipleship

Lord, thank you for your Word which is a lamp unto my feet and a light unto my path.[1] I will study it diligently so that I will be approved by you. I want to be your disciple, without any shame.[2]

Through your grace, Father, I will let the Word of Christ dwell richly within me, in all wisdom, as I teach and admonish others with Scriptures and expressions of truth in all forms. Whatever I do as a disciple of Jesus Christ, I will do in His name, giving thanks to you, Father.[3]

Lord, I will bless you at all times. Your praise shall continually be in my mouth. My soul shall make its boast in you, and as I do this, the humble will hear me and this will gladden their hearts. When I sought you, Lord, you heard me, and you delivered me from all my fears.[4] Therefore, I am privileged to be a disciple of Jesus Christ.

Through your assistance, I will speak of your righteousness and sing your praises all day long.[5] As a disciple of Jesus Christ, I willingly take up my cross, denying myself, and following Him.[6] His way is perfect.[7]

References: (1) Psalms 119:105; (2) 2 Timothy 2:15; (3) Colossians 3:16-17; (4) Psalms 34:1-4; (5) Psalms 35:28; (6) Luke 9:23-24; (7) Psalms 18:30.

22. Discipline

Key Promise: *"If ye endure chastening, God dealeth with you as with sons; for what son is he whom the father chasteneth not?" (Heb. 12:7).*

Discipline stems from a word that means follower, adherent, or student. A disciple of Jesus Christ adheres to the discipline (or teaching) of His Master.

Sometimes, it is important to realize, teaching requires correction, as when a student takes a test and the teacher corrects it by giving proper credit for right answers and pointing out the errors. The Lord's discipline in our lives works in much the same way. It is important to remember that its purpose is to help us grow into mature, responsible believers.

When we face a test in life, we may make mistakes in the way we handle the test. It becomes necessary, therefore, for our Master to correct us so that we can get up and try again. If we need extra help, all we need to do is go to Him in prayer and to let His Word speak to our hearts.

As disciples of the Master, therefore, we can expect His loving correction in our lives. If we make the wise decision to learn from it, we will experience greater peace, joy, and righteousness in our lives.

Promise-Prayer of Discipline

Heavenly Father, I beseech you to give me the grace I need to endure your discipline in my life. I realize it is good for me, and that you will deal with me as your child.[1] Thank you, Lord.

Correct me as needed, Father, so that my heart will be perfect before you. I want to faithfully walk according to your statutes and to always keep your commandments.[2] Enable me, Lord, to be a doer of your Word, not just a hearer.[3] I want to be your treasure, Father; therefore, I will obey your voice and keep your covenant.[4]

With your help, I will walk in obedience at all times, because I love you with all my heart.[5] Guide me through the process that equips me to cast down imaginations and every high thing that exalts itself against knowing you, Father. Help me bring into captivity my every thought to the obedience of Christ.[6]

Lord, I am willing to be obedient at all times. Teach me your way.[7] It is wonderful to know that you reward obedience with the good of the land.[8] I receive your correction, Father, because I know it comes from your love for me.[9]

References: *(1) Hebrews 12:7; (2) 1 Kings 8:61; (3) James 1:22; (4) Exodus 19:5; (5) John 14:15; (6) 2 Corinthians 10:5; (7) Psalms 25:4; (8) Deuteronomy 28:11; (9) Hebrews 12:6.*

23. Discovery

Key Promise: *"By faith Abraham, when he was called to go out into a place which he should after receive for an inheritance, obeyed; and he went out, not knowing whither he went. By faith he sojourned in the land of promise, as in a strange country, ... For he looked for a city which hath foundations, whose builder and maker is God" (Heb. 11:8-11).*

We begin the journey of faith with a discovery of who we are. "For all have sinned and fall short of the glory of God" (Rom. 3:23, NKJV). We discover that we are needy sinners.

The next discovery is a discovery of who Jesus is — our personal Savior and Lord. It was He who said, "I am the way, the truth, and the life. No one comes to the Father except through Me" (John 14:6, NKJV).

The love of God — perhaps the best discovery of all — then dawns upon us: "But God demonstrates His own love toward us, in that while we were still sinners, Christ died for us" (Rom. 5:8, NKJV).

From then on, it is one amazing discovery after another as God gives us spiritual understanding through His Word. For example, we learn that we have eternal life: "For the wages of sin is death, but the gift of God is eternal life in Christ Jesus our Lord" (Rom. 6:23, NKJV).

Every day is your day of discovery.

Promise-Prayer of Discovery

Father, your hands have made me and fashioned me. Please impart your understanding to my heart so that I will learn to obey all your commandments, Lord.[1] Through your precepts and promises I gain new understandings that cause me to hate every false way I find in the world.[2]

Impart your wisdom to me, Father. I know you give liberally to me.[3] I want to discover your wisdom in all its fullness, and I never want to forget what you reveal to me.

With your help, Lord, I will never forsake the discoveries you reveal to me, because I know your truth and your wisdom will preserve me. I love the discoveries you keep on revealing to me, and I know that these spiritual discoveries will keep me.[4] Thank you, Father.

Discovering your wisdom is the principal thing I seek, Lord.[5] The discoveries it brings to me preserve me and keep me.[6] The understanding you impart to me is a wellspring of life to me, Father.[7]

References: (1) Psalms 119:73; (2) Psalms 119:104; (3) James 1:5; (4) Proverbs 4:5-6; (5) Proverbs 4:7; (6) Proverbs 2:11; (7) Proverbs 9:6.

24. Endurance

Key Promise: *"Behold, we count them happy which endure. Ye have heard of the patience of Job, and have seen the end of the Lord; that the Lord is very pitiful, and of tender mercy" (James 5:11).*

Endurance is a quality of life that enables us to keep on keeping on. Many wonderful promises are extended to those who will endure.

Endurance enables us to conquer temptation. James points out, "Blessed is the man that endureth temptation: for when he is tried, he shall receive the crown of life, which the Lord hath promised to them that love him" (James 1:12).

Endurance enables us to receive God's promises: "Therefore do not cast away your confidence, which has great reward. For you have need of endurance, so that after you have done the will of God, you may receive the promise" (Heb. 10:35-36, NKJV).

Endurance helps us to keep on running the race that God has set before us. "Therefore we also, since we are surrounded by so great a cloud of witnesses, let us lay aside every weight, and the sin which so easily ensnares us, and let us run with endurance the race that is set before us, looking unto Jesus, the author and finisher of our faith, who for the joy that was set before Him endured the cross, despising the shame, and has sat down at the right hand of the throne of God" (Heb. 12:1-2, NKJV).

Promise-Prayer of Endurance

With your help, Lord, I will keep on keeping on so that I might walk worthy of you unto all pleasing. Make me fruitful in every good work, and help me to increase in my knowledge of you. You are strengthening me with all might according to your glorious power. You are granting me patience with joyfulness, and this enables me to endure. For these reasons, Father, I give you thanks. You have made it possible for me to be a partaker of your inheritance.[1]

Therefore, I will lay aside every weight and every besetting sin. Through your grace, I will run with patient endurance the race you have set before me. I will keep looking to Jesus who is the Author and Finisher of my faith.[2] How I thank you, Father, that you gave your only begotten Son to save me.[3] For the joy that was set before Him, He endured the cross in my behalf, and now He is sitting at your right hand.[4] Thank you for His great example of endurance, Lord. I can do all things through Him.[5]

References: (1) Colossians 1:1-12; (2) Hebrews 12:1-2; (3) John 3:16; (4) Hebrews 12:2; (5) Philippians 4:13.

25. Enthusiasm

Key Promise: *"Whom [Jesus Christ] having not seen, ye love; in whom, though now ye see him not, yet believing, ye rejoice with joy unspeakable and full of glory" (1 Pet. 1:8).*

Enthusiasm always characterizes a believer's life because this important word literally means "to be inspired by God." In fact, the dictionary states that enthusiasm is "belief in special revelations of the Holy Spirit." It also defines enthusiasm as "strong excitement of feeling; something inspiring zeal or fervor."

It is true that people frequently feel free to get excited about almost anything except their religious faith. It is as if enthusiasm over the things of God is not permitted.

An anonymous writer observed, "An enthusiastic approach to religion is preferable to mere religious formalism which is purely aesthetic and orderly but lacking in dynamic power. The need today is for a relevant and vibrant Christianity that will summon one's whole enthusiasm."

We need to remember the words of the Prophet Nehemiah who wrote about enthusiasm thusly: "The joy of the Lord is your strength" (Neh. 8:10). The Scriptures make it very clear that God desires His people to be joyful — full of enthusiasm about their faith.

Promise-Prayer of Enthusiasm

Truly, Lord, your joy is my strength.[1] I will walk in your joy, Father, because I know that a merry heart brings healing to me that is far better than any medicine. I feel enthused and infused with your power, Lord, when I realize that your kingdom does not consist of meat and drink, but it is made up of righteousness, peace, and joy in the Holy Spirit.[2]

Thank you for making my heart merry and full of enthusiasm for you. Wherever I go I will reflect that enthusiasm with a cheerful countenance.[3] Father, you have restored unto me the joy of my salvation and you have upheld me with your free Spirit. Therefore, I will enthusiastically teach your ways and your Word to transgressors so that sinners will be converted unto you.[4]

The promises of your Word fill me with excitement and enthusiasm, Father, and that enthusiasm impels me to reach out to others. Because I love righteousness and hate wickedness you have anointed me with the oil of gladness.[5] Thank you for the enthusiasm your promises impart to me, Lord.

References: (1) Nehemiah 8:10; (2) Romans 14:17-18; (3) Proverbs 15:13; (4) Psalms 51:12-13; (5) Psalms 45:7.

26. Evangelism

Key Promise: *"The Lord is not slack concerning his promise, as some men count slackness; but is longsuffering to usward, not willing that any should perish, but that all should come to repentance" (2 Pet. 3:9).*

Evangelism comes from a Greek word *evangel*, which means good news. An evangelist is one who shares the Good News of Jesus Christ with others, and evangelism is the practice of sharing the Good News wherever we go.

The power to be an effective witness for Jesus Christ comes from the Holy Spirit. Jesus promised, "But ye shall receive power, after that the Holy Ghost is come upon you: and ye shall be witnesses unto me" (Acts 1:8). The word *power* here comes from a Greek root *dunamis*, which has become the basis for English words such as dynamic, dynamo, and dynamite. Through the Holy Spirit, God has unleashed dynamic power in our lives to enable us to be dynamic witnesses for Jesus Christ.

"The Lord is not slack concerning his promise, as some men count slackness; but is longsuffering to usward, not willing that any should perish, but that all should come to repentance" (2 Pet. 3:9). Realizing this, we are ready to share the Good News with all.

Promise-Prayer of Evangelism

Lord God, I sanctify you in my heart, and this enables me to be always ready to give an answer to anyone who asks me about my faith.[1] I will study your Word with diligence so that I can be approved unto you, a workman who never needs to be ashamed.[2] Lead me to those who need to know you.

I will fill my heart with your Word, Lord, so that I might not sin against you.[3] This will fill my heart with your good treasures, enabling me to bring forth that which is good so that others will receive your Word with openness and eagerness. I realize, Lord, that it is out of the abundance of my heart that I speak,[4] and I want the abundance of my heart to be based upon the precious promises of your Word.

I will meditate upon your Word, settling your promises in my heart, so that I will be able to speak words of faith and life to others.[5] It causes my heart to rejoice with the angels of heaven, Lord, whenever I am privileged to lead a lost soul to you.[6] Help me to do so faithfully.

References: (1) 1 Peter 3:15; (2) 2 Timothy 2:15; (3) Psalms 119:11; (4) Luke 6:45; (5) Luke 21:14; (6) Luke 15:4-7.

27. Everlasting Life

Key Promise: *"He that hath the Son hath life; and he that hath not the Son of God hath not life" (1 John 5:12).*

To realize that God has given to us everlasting life — a life that never ends — is to realize how much He loves us. "For God so loved the world that He gave His only begotten Son, that whoever believes in Him should not perish but have everlasting life" (John 3:16, NKJV).

Alexander Whyte would echo the evangelistic cry of his heart at the close of many sermons. He would raise two rhetorical questions about heaven. First, he would often ask, "What will it be to be there?" Then he would follow that question with another: "Aye, and what will it be not to be there?"

The Bible says, "Therefore we do not lose heart. Even though our outward man is perishing, yet the inward man is being renewed day by day. For our light affliction, which is but for a moment, is working for us a far more exceeding and eternal weight of glory, while we do not look at the things which are seen, but at the things which are not seen. For the things which are seen are temporary, but the things which are not seen are eternal" (2 Cor. 4:16-18, NKJV).

Knowing that God has given eternal life to me makes me realize how important it is for me to live life fully in the here-and-now.

Promise-Prayer of Everlasting Life

Through your grace, Father, I will not let my heart be troubled, because I believe in you, Lord, and I trust every promise of your Word. I believe in Jesus Christ as my personal Savior and Lord. Father, in your house there are many mansions. I know this because Jesus assures me that He has gone to prepare a place for me so that I can be with Him through all eternity. How I look forward to taking up occupancy of the eternal quarters He has prepared for me.[1]

It thrills me to know that Jesus is coming back to earth in order to receive me unto himself.[2] What a wonderful Lord He is. He is the way, the truth, and the life to me.[3] Jesus is the Bread of Life to me. I have partaken of His life by eating the Bread of Life, and He promises me that I will live forever. Thank you, Father, for this promise.[4]

Most of all, Father, I want to thank you that you commended your love toward me when I was yet a sinner by sending your Son to die for me.[5] You loved me so much that you willingly sacrificed your only begotten Son for me, and now, because I believe in Him, I know that I will not perish, but have everlasting life.[6] Thank you so much, Father-God.

Everlasting life with you is the fulfillment of my greatest dream.

References: (1) John 14:1-3; (2) John 14:3; (3) John 14:6; (4) John 6:48-51; (5) Romans 5:8; (6) John 3:16.

28. Faith

Key Promise: *"For whatsoever is born of God overcometh the world: and this is the victory that overcometh the world, even our faith"* (1 John 5:4).

The best definition of faith that was ever written is found in the Bible: "Now faith is the substance of things hoped for, the evidence of things not seen" (Heb. 11:1). Our faith pleases the heart of God: "But without faith it is impossible to please him: for he that cometh to God must believe that he is, and that he is a rewarder of them that diligently seek him" (Heb. 11:6).

Faith firmly states, "If God be for us, who can be against us" (Rom. 8:31).

Faith believes, "With God nothing shall be impossible" (Luke 1:37).

Faith claims God's promises. Faith holds onto truth. Faith reaches out to God for all He has in store: "Now unto him that is able to do exceeding abundantly above all that we ask or think, according to the power that worketh in us" (Eph. 3:20).

Faith saves the sick. (See James 5:15.) The shield of faith quenches all the fiery darts of the wicked. (See Eph. 6:16.)

Read God's Word and build your faith. (See Rom. 10:17.) Pray God's promises and receive His answers.

Promise-Prayer of Faith

Heavenly Father, thank you for the power of faith in my life. I have been saved by faith in your grace.[1] Thank you for always rewarding my faith.[2] Even though I've never seen Jesus, faith enables me to love Him, and in Him I rejoice with exceeding joy, because I know that the end of my faith will be the salvation of my soul.[3]

I believe all the promises of your Word, Lord. I believe that nothing is impossible with you.[4] I believe that nothing is too hard for you.[5] I believe I will receive your promises, Father.[6] Help me to live according to your faith, Lord.[7]

Help me to always walk by faith, not by sight.[8] I will lay aside every weight and every besetting sin so that I can run with endurance the race you have set before me, Lord. I will keep on looking to Jesus who is the Author and Finisher of my faith.[9] For the joy that was set before Him He endured the cross in my behalf, and now He is seated next to you, Father.[10] Thank you for the ability to claim all your promises through faith.

References: *(1) Ephesians 2:8-9; (2) Hebrews 11:6; (3) 1 Peter 1:8-9; (4) Luke 1:37; (5) Jeremiah 32:27; (6) Hebrews 10:36; (7) Habakkuk 2:4; (8) 2 Corinthians 5:7; (9) Hebrews 12:1; (10) Hebrews 12:2.*

29. Faithfulness of God

Key Promise: *"Faithful is he that calleth you, who also will do it" (1 Thess. 5:24).*

God is the great Promise-keeper, and we can be promise-reapers if we will trust Him to fulfill His Word in our lives.

If God said it, we can count on it. He never lies. In fact, there is only one thing that God cannot do, and that is to fail. He and His Word are completely trustworthy in every respect, and that is why it behooves us to pray His promises with trust and confidence.

Some of God's promises related to His faithfulness are cited below:

"Faithful is he that calleth you, who also will do it" (1 Thess. 5:24).

"God is faithful, by whom ye were called unto the fellowship of his Son Jesus Christ our Lord" (1 Cor. 1:9).

"As for God, his way is perfect: the word of the Lord is tried: he is a buckler to all those that trust in him" (Ps. 18:30).

"So shall my word be that goeth forth out of my mouth: it shall not return unto me void, but it shall accomplish that which I please, and its shall prosper in the thing whereto I sent it" (Isa. 55:11).

Promise-Prayer of God's Faithfulness

Lord God, thank you for your great faithfulness in my life. Morning by morning and day by day I see your hand at work. Your mercies are always available to me, because your compassion for me never fails. Great is your faithfulness to me, O Father.[1]

Father, I know you are watching out for me. You never slumber nor sleep, and you will never permit my foot to be moved.[2] Thank you, Lord. All of your promises are yes, and they are amen.[3]

Thank you for being ever ready to perform your Word in my life.[4] I know that all the temptations that come my way are common to people everywhere. Thank you, Lord, for your faithfulness which will not permit me to ever be tempted beyond my ability to endure.[5]

Your Word declares that you will never leave me nor forsake me.[6] Nothing can ever separate me from your love.[7]

The knowledge of your faithfulness in my life fills me with a complete sense of security. Thank you, Father.

I trust you with everything I am and have.

References: (1) Lamentations 3:23; (2) Psalms 121:3-4; (3) 2 Corinthians 1:20; (4) Jeremiah 1:12; (5) 1 Corinthians 10:13; (6) Hebrews 13:5; (7) Romans 8:39.

30. Fatherhood of God

Key Promise: *"Thou, O Lord, art our father, our redeemer; thy name is from everlasting" (Isa. 63:16).*

God is our heavenly Father. He loves us with a father's heart. The Bible says, "Your Father knoweth what things ye have need of, before ye ask him" (Matt. 6:8). This statement of faith is part of Jesus' wonderful Sermon on the Mount, and it precedes His model prayer, which begins: "Our Father which art in heaven, Hallowed by thy name . . . " (Matt. 6:9-13).

There is one God, and He is our Father. That's a tremendous thought in and of itself! The Bible says, "There is one God, the Father, of whom are all things, and we for Him; and one Lord Jesus Christ, through whom are all things, and through whom we live" (1 Cor. 8:6, NKJV). One God. One Father. And one Lord Jesus Christ. Through Him, we are able to get to know God.

Jesus said, "I am the way, the truth, and the life. No one comes to the Father except through Me. If you had known Me, you would have known My Father also; and from now on you know Him and have seen Him" (John 14:6-7, NKJV). There is only one way to get to know our heavenly Father, and that is by getting to know Jesus, as He is revealed in the Word.

Promise-Prayer of God's Fatherhood

Heavenly Father, I come boldly to the throne of grace where I know I will find your mercy and grace which will help me with every need of my life.[1] I thank you for your promise that you will be a Father to the fatherless, and I claim this promise for my life, because I know I need your Fatherhood in my life.[2]

You have enlightened the eyes of my understanding so that I am able to know the hope of your calling and the riches of the glory of your inheritance in my life. Thank you, Father, for the exceeding greatness of your power toward me.[3] You are so rich in mercy, and I continue to be amazed by your great love which you have so freely bestowed on me.[4]

I want to imitate you, Father, by walking in love, as Christ has loved me and given himself for me.[5] Father, I thank you for your promise that you will supply all my needs according to your riches in glory by Christ Jesus.[6] As I draw near to you, Father, I know you are drawing near to me.[7]

References: (1) Hebrews 4:16; (2) Psalms 68:5; (3) Ephesians 1:19; (4) Ephesians 2:4; (5) Ephesians 5:1-2; (6) Philippians 4:19; (7) James 4:8.

31. Forgiveness

Key Promise: *"For if ye forgive men their trespasses, your heavenly Father will also forgive you: But if ye forgive not men their trespasses, neither will your Father forgive your trespasses"* (Matt. 6:14-15).

The Bible is a book of forgiveness that tells us, "If we confess our sins, he is faithful and just to forgive us our sins, and to cleanse us from all unrighteousness" (1 John 1:9).

Jesus prayed, "Give us this day our daily bread. And forgive us our debts, as we forgive our debtors" (Matt. 6:11-12). This well-known plea comes from the Lord's Prayer, and immediately afterward Jesus said, "For if ye forgive men their trespasses, your heavenly Father will also forgive you" (Matt. 6:14-15).

As we reflect on the teaching of Jesus, we see a direct relationship between our capacity to forgive others and God's willingness to forgive us. When we pray, "Forgive our trespasses as we forgive those who trespass against us," do we really want God to forgive us in the same way we show forgiveness to others? This would be our true prayer only if we knew there was no unforgiveness in our heart toward others.

Jesus reminds us, "Her sins, which are many, are forgiven; for she loved much: but to whom little is forgiven, the same loveth little" (Luke 7:47). Clearly, the ability to forgive stems from the ability to love, and we love ". . . because he [Jesus] first loved us" (1 John 4:19).

Promise-Prayer of Forgiveness

Father-God, thank you for the blessings that forgiveness brings into my life. You have made me accepted in the beloved, because of Christ's atoning work on the cross. Thank you, Lord, for the redemption you have provided for me through His blood and the forgiveness of my sins according to the riches of your grace.[1]

You have forgiven all my iniquities, and I praise your holy name.[2] Thank you for removing my transgressions from me as far as the east is from the west.[3] You have been merciful toward my unrighteousness, and you have chosen to forget my sins.[4] Thank you, Father. Therefore, I will forsake all sinfulness, and I will remain with you, Lord. Have mercy upon me, I pray. Thank you for your abundant pardon in my life.[5]

Help me to forgive others as you have forgiven me.[6] Through your grace I will forgive others and I will forbear with others in the same way that Christ has forgiven me.[7] When I stand praying, I will forgive so that you, Father, will forgive me.[8]

As I confess my sins to you, I know you are forgiving me and cleansing me from all unrighteousness.[9]

References: *(1) Ephesians 1:6-7; (2) Psalms 85:2; (3) Psalms 103:12; (4) Hebrews 8:12; (5) Isaiah 55:7; (6) Matthew 6:12-18; (7) Colossians 3:13; (8) Mark 11:25; (9) 1 John 1:9.*

32. Fortitude

Key Promise: *"That he would grant you, according to the riches of his glory, to be strengthened with might by his Spirit in the inner man; That Christ may dwell in your hearts by faith; that ye, being rooted and grounded in love, may be able to comprehend with all saints what is the breadth, and length, and depth, and height; And to know the love of Christ, which passeth knowledge, that ye might be filled with all the fulness of God" (Eph. 3:16-19).*

Fortitude is a quality of inner strength. The believer is strengthened with might by the indwelling Holy Spirit. This results in fortitude that faces all fear with faith.

We are strong in the Lord, and ". . . in the power of His might" (Eph. 6:10). His strength is made perfect in our weakness. (See 2 Cor. 12:9.) Fortitude comes from waiting on the Lord, as Isaiah pointed out, "They that wait upon the Lord shall renew their strength" (Isa. 40:31).

True fortitude is described by Paul in his great passage on spiritual warfare. He admonishes us to put on the whole armor of God: ". . . that ye may be able to stand against the wiles of the devil. For we wrestle not against flesh and blood, but against principalities, against powers, against the rulers of the darkness of this world, against spiritual wickedness in high places" (Eph. 6:11-12).

Promise-Prayer of Fortitude

God, thank you for giving me strength at all times. You have always strengthened me.[1] Continue to strengthen me according to the promises of your Word.[2] With your help, Lord, I will walk worthy of you. I want to please you at all times, and to be fruitful in every good work as I grow in my knowledge of you. Thank you for strengthening me with all might, according to your glorious power, unto all patience and longsuffering with joyfulness. For all these blessings, Father, I give you thanks. I rejoice in the knowledge that you have made me capable of being a receiver of your inheritance.[3]

You give me fortitude and you increase my strength.[4] Lord, you are my rock and my fortress. You are my Deliverer, my strength, and my God. I trust you implicitly, because you are my buckler and the horn of my salvation. Thank you for being my high tower into whom I can run and find refuge.[5]

Your Word gives me fortitude, Father, as I reflect upon and pray your promises, because your Word is quick and powerful.[6] Because you are my light and my salvation, Lord, I will fear no one and no thing. You are the strength of my life; therefore, I will not fear.[7]

References: (1) Daniel 10:19; (2) Psalms 119:28; (3) Colossians 1:10-12; (4) Isaiah 40:29; (5) Psalms 18:2; (6) Hebrews 4:12; (7) Psalms 27:1.

33. Freedom

Key Promise: *"And ye shall know the truth, and the truth shall make you free"* (John 8:32).

The Bible is the believer's Emancipation Proclamation. It promises us that God will free us from Satan, sin, and all forms of evil. Our responsibility is to believe God's Word and to stand fast. Paul wrote, "Stand fast therefore in the liberty wherewith Christ hath made us free, and be not entangled again with the yoke of bondage" (Gal. 5:1).

A gospel song tells the story clearly. We're free from the fear of tomorrow and from the guilt of the past. We've traded our chains for a glorious song. And we're free at last. The Father has called us to liberty. His freedom is there for us to enjoy, but its purpose is not a selfish one. The freedom God imparts to the believer motivates us to love and serve others. (See Gal. 5:13.)

The Spirit of the Lord is a Spirit of liberty, and where the Spirit is there is liberty — the glorious liberty of the children of God. (See 2 Cor. 3:17.)

Because of God's great gift of liberty in our lives, we are able to say with Paul, "There is therefore now no condemnation to them which are in Christ Jesus, who walk not after the flesh, but after the Spirit. For the law of the Spirit of life in Christ Jesus hath made me free from the law of sin and death" (Rom. 8:1-2).

Now that's freedom!

Promise-Prayer of Freedom

Lord, thank you for your Word of truth[1] and the Spirit of truth[2] which have made me free.[3] How I praise you, Father, for the law of the Spirit of life in Christ Jesus that has set me free from the law of sin and death.[4] With your help, I will stand fast in the liberty wherewith you have set me free, and I will not permit myself to ever again be entangled with a yoke of bondage.[5]

Thank you for saving me from my sin.[6] I believe in your Son, my Lord and Savior, Jesus Christ, who willingly gave His life as a sacrifice for my sins.[7] You have revealed Him to be the Lamb of God who takes away the sins of the world.[8] Thank you for justifying me freely by your grace through the redemption that Jesus Christ has provided for me.[9] This is what enables me to enter into the glorious liberty of your children[10] which I now enjoy.

I am truly free, Father, and I will not use my liberty as a cloak of evil conduct, but as your servant, Lord.[11] I am so thankful for your gift of liberty in my life, and I will walk in that freedom because I am truly free.[12]

References: (1) John 17:17; (2) John 14:17; (3) John 8:32; (4) Romans 8:1-2; (5) Galatians 5:1; (6) Romans 6:23; (7) Romans 3:25; (8) John 1:29; (9) Romans 3:24; (10) Romans 8:21; (11) 1 Peter 2:16; (12) Galatians 5:1.

34. Future

Key Promise: *"Surely goodness and mercy shall follow me all the days of my life: and I will dwell in the house of the Lord for ever"* (Ps. 23:6).

There is no need to fear the future, because God's ". . . perfect love casteth out fear" (1 John 4:18). Jesus does not want us to ever worry about the future. In fact, He admonishes us, "Take therefore no thought for the morrow: for the morrow shall take thought for the things of itself. Sufficient unto the day is the evil thereof" (Matt. 6:34).

Instead of worrying about the future, we should keep our focus on the things of God, because Jesus promises, "Let not your heart be troubled: ye believe in God, believe also in me. In my Father's house are many mansions: if it were not so, I would have told you. I go to prepare a place for you. And if I go and prepare a place for you, I will come again, and receive you unto myself; that where I am, there ye may be also" (John 14:1-3).

That's the end of the story! That's our ultimate future as believers! Goodness and mercy will follow us all the days of our lives and we will dwell in the house of the Lord forever. (See Ps. 23:6.)

Promise-Prayer for the Future

Lord God, thank you for all the promises of your Word concerning my future. I believe them and I receive them by faith. Thank you for the record of your Word that assures me that I have eternal life.[1] I'm so glad to know that my spirit will live forever with you.[2]

Thank you, Lord, for making death like a shadowy illusion to me.[3] It no longer has any sting, and the grave will not be victorious over me.[4] My heart is filled with gratitude when I realize that Jesus is the resurrection and the life to me. I believe in Him, and because I do, Father, you have made it possible for me to live after death.[5]

Until that day, Lord, I will trust in you with all my heart, leaning not to my own understanding. In all my ways I will acknowledge you, and I know that you will direct my paths.[6]

I believe your Word, Lord, and because I do I am able to face the future without fear. Thank you, Father.

References: (1) 1 John 5:11; (2) Psalms 22:26; (3) Psalms 23:4; (4) 1 Corinthians 15:55; (5) John 11:25; (6) Proverbs 3:5-6.

35. Giving

Key Promise: *"Give, and it shall be given unto you; good measure, pressed down, and shaken together, and running over, shall men give into your bosom. For with the same measure that ye mete withal it shall be measured to you again" (Luke 6:38).*

It is only what we give away that we shall be able to keep for all eternity. The things we cling to on this earth will not go with us into heaven. Therefore, it is wise for us to keep our focus on the things that have eternal value.

Jesus said, "Lay not up for yourselves treasures upon earth, where moth and rust doth corrupt, and where thieves break through and steal: But lay up for yourselves treasures in heaven, where neither moth nor rust doth corrupt, and where thieves do not break through nor steal: For where your treasure is, there will your heart be also" (Matt. 6:19-21).

While we make a living by what we get, we make a life by what we give. It may be possible to give without loving, but it is totally impossible to love without giving. God never fails to make a note of our generosity, even if the world may not thank us.

The Bible says, "Every man according as he purposeth in his heart, so let him give; not grudgingly, or of necessity: for God loveth a cheerful giver" (2 Cor. 9:7).

Promise-Prayer of Giving

I believe your Word, Father, which tells me that you will make me plenteous in goods. You will give me your treasure and you will bless the work of my hands. Because these promises are true, I will be able to give freely, and you will make me the head, not the tail. You will put me above, not underneath. I will obey your commandments, Father. I will observe and do your Word.[1]

Even as I pray, Lord, I sense that the blessings you have provided for me are overtaking me, because I am hearkening to your voice. I know I will be blessed in the city, and I will be blessed in the field. All that I am and have shall be blessed by your hand. My possessions and my supplies are being blessed by you. I am blessed when I come in and I am blessed when I go out. You will cause all my enemies to be smitten. They will flee from me in seven different directions.[2] O Lord, I love you.

Thank you, Lord, for commanding these blessings upon me, and for blessing me in the land you've given unto me.[3] Because of your blessing, I will give. The more I give the more I receive from you. Thank you, Father, for the good measure you give. It is pressed down, shaken together, and running over.[4] My heart pumps with gratitude to you, Father.

References: (1) Deuteronomy 28:11-13; (2) Deuteronomy 28:2-7; (3) Deuteronomy 28:8; (4) Luke 6:38.

36. Grace

Key Promise: *"God is able to make all grace abound toward you" (2 Cor. 9:8).*

God's grace is an all-sufficient grace that is made operable in our lives through faith. "And he said unto me, My grace is sufficient for thee: for my strength is made perfect in weakness. Most gladly therefore will I rather glory in my infirmities, that the power of Christ may rest upon me" (2 Cor. 12:9).

E. Stanley Jones wrote, "Grace binds you with far stronger cords than the cords of duty or obligation can bind you. Grace is free, but when once you take it you are bound forever to the Giver, and bound to catch the spirit of the Giver. Like produces like. Grace makes you gracious, the Giver makes you give."

We do not merit God's grace. He extends it to us freely in response to our faith. Our Christian life begins as a work of grace. "For by grace are ye saved through faith; and that not of yourselves: it is the gift of God: Not of works, lest any man should boast" (Eph 2:8-9).

Robert Louis Stevenson wrote, "There is nothing but God's grace. We walk upon it; we breathe it; we live and die by it." God promises His grace to be with us every day of our lives, and we appropriate His grace by faith through prayer.

Promise-Prayer of Grace

Heavenly Father, thank you for your all-sufficient grace. It is wonderful to know that you perfect your grace during my times of weakness.[1] You are able to make all of your grace abound in my life.[2] I richly enjoy your abundant, amazing grace in my life.[3]

While I was yet a sinner your love reached down and claimed me to be your adopted child. Thank you, Father, for the blood of Jesus that cleansed me and freed me from sin.[4] Whereas sin once abounded in my life, your grace now abounds far more.[5]

Help me, Lord, to grow in the grace and knowledge of my Lord and Savior Jesus Christ.[6] The measure of grace you have given to me is sustaining me at all times.[7] Thank you for justifying me by your grace.[8] Therefore, I ask you to help me be strong in the grace that is in Christ Jesus.[9] Thank you, Father.

Because of your mercy and grace, Father, my peace is constantly being multiplied.[10] Now I know that the inheritance you have bequeathed to me is incorruptible and undefiled. It will never fade away, because you have reserved it in heaven for me.[11] Thank you, Lord, for the power of your grace which always keeps me.[12]

References: *(1) 2 Corinthians 12:9; (2) 2 Corinthians 9:8; (3) 2 Corinthians 4:15; (4) Romans 5:8; (5) Romans 5:20; (6) 2 Peter 3:18; (7) Ephesians 4:7; (8) Titus 3:7; (9) 2 Timothy 2:1; (10) 2 Peter 1:2; (11) 1 Peter 1:4; (12) 1 Peter 1:5.*

37. Growth

Key Promise: *"The righteous shall flourish like the palm tree: he shall grow like a cedar in Lebanon"* (Ps. 92:12).

Hannah Whitall Smith observed, "The mother eagle teaches her little ones to fly by making their nest so uncomfortable that they are forced to leave it and commit themselves to the unknown world of air outside. And just so does our God to us. He stirs up our comfortable nests, and pushes us over the edge of them, and we are forced to use our wings to save ourselves from fatal falling. Read your trials in this light, and see if you cannot begin to get a glimpse of their meaning. Your wings are being developed."

This kind of growth happens to us when we: "Let the word of Christ dwell in you richly in all wisdom; teaching and admonishing one another in psalms and hymns and spiritual songs, singing with grace in your hearts to the Lord" (Col. 3:16). The goal is spiritual maturity as it is outlined by Paul: "That we henceforth be no more children, tossed to and fro, and carried about with every wind of doctrine, by the sleight of men, and cunning craftiness, whereby they lie in wait to deceive; But speaking the truth in love, may grow up into him in all things, which is the head, even Christ" (Eph. 4:14-15).

Spiritual growth in the Christian life is the fulfillment of our responsibilities as children of the King, and praying God's promises helps us to find this degree of maturity.

Promise-Prayer of Growth

As I behold your glory, Lord, I thank you that you are changing me from glory to glory by your Spirit at work in my life.[1] I have great confidence, Lord, that you are continuing your workmanship in my life.[2] Help my love to abound more and more as I walk in the knowledge of your Word.[3] With your help, Father, I will be able to approve things that are excellent, and I will be sincere and without offense until the day of Christ.[4]

Thank you for the riches of your glory in my life. Grant me, according to your riches, that I would be strengthened with might by your Spirit in my inner being. It's wonderful to know, Lord, that Christ dwells in my heart by faith, and He is rooting me and grounding me in love so that I will be able to comprehend with all saints the breadth, length, depth, and height of your love. Keep on filling me, Father, with all your fullness.[5]

As a newborn babe, I desire the sincere milk of your Word so that I may grow strong and tall in your kingdom, Lord.[6]

Thank you for always helping me to grow, Father.

References: (1) 2 Corinthians 3:18; (2) Philippians 1:6; (3) Philippians 1:9; (4) Philippians 1:10; (5) Ephesians 3:14-19; (6) 1 Peter 2:2-3.

38. Guidance

Key Promise: *"Thy word is a lamp unto my feet, and a light unto my path"* (Ps. 119:105).

God knows our nature as no one else does. God knows the future as no one else does. God has a purpose for our lives. These three reasons reveal why we need God's daily guidance in our lives.

God's Word is a guidebook for life. If we let God guide us, He will provide for us each step of the way. "As many as are led by the Spirit of God, they are the sons of God" (Rom. 8:14).

G. Campbell Morgan wrote, "When we fear that we may not know the meaning of God's will, we had better turn to himself for clear guidance and safekeeping." God reveals His will to us through the promises of His Word. Those promises are His will for us. If we will focus on the promises instead of the problems His will shall come to pass in our lives.

A trainer of seeing-eye dogs advised a blind student, "Walk closer to him. The dog cannot guide you if you keep him at arm's length." It is the same with God's guidance in our lives. We must draw ever closer to Him through prayer and the study of His Word.

Divine guidance is not a spiritual luxury; it is a minimum necessity for every believer. We cannot expect Him to guide us unless His will, not our own, is the supreme purpose of our lives.

Promise-Prayer of Guidance

Thank you for your Word, Father. It is a lamp unto my feet and a light unto my path.[1] When I go anywhere, your Word leads me. When I am sleeping, it keeps me. When I awaken, it talks with me. Your Word is a lamp, and your law is a light. Your instructions are the way of life I have chosen to follow.[2]

Help me to keep your Word in my heart so that I will not sin against you, Lord.[3] Help me to keep your Word in my mouth as well so that I will be able to meditate upon your promises day and night. With your help, Father, I will observe to do according to all your Word, because I know that following your Word is the pathway to prosperity and success.[4] Thank you for the guidance your Word gives to me.

I will depend upon the Holy Spirit to guide me,[5] and I will listen for your directing voice at all times, Father, and I know you will reveal your way to me. In times of indecision, I know you will say to me, "This is the way, walk ye in it." This fact will keep me from ever turning to the right or the left.[6]

Your exceeding great and precious promises are my life, Lord.[7]

References: (1) Psalms 119:105; (2) Proverbs 6:22-23; (3) Psalms 119:11; (4) Joshua 1:8; (5) Romans 8:14; (6) Isaiah 30:21; (7) 2 Peter 1:4.

39. Happiness

Key Promise: *"A merry heart maketh a cheerful countenance: but by sorrow of the heart the spirit is broken" (Prov. 15:13).*

The Bible says, "Thou lovest righteousness, and hatest wickedness: therefore God, thy God, hath anointed thee with the oil of gladness above thy fellows. All thy garments smell of myrrh, and aloes, and cassia, out of the ivory palaces, whereby they have made thee glad" (Ps. 45:7-8).

The connection between righteousness and happiness is profound, and righteousness is something God imparts to us through faith in Jesus Christ. Happiness is not something you have in your hands; it is something you carry in your heart. Yes, true happiness comes from within. It is in your heart, not in the circumstances surrounding you.

Therefore, we can say with certainty that happiness is an attitude that comes from realizing the indwelling presence of God's Holy Spirit. In God's presence there is fullness of joy. (See Ps. 16:11.)

The place to be happy is here. The time to be happy is now. The way to be happy is to make others so. Happiness is not perfected unless it is shared with others. Too many people are concerned with what they think life "owes them." The happy person is concerned with what he or she owes life. Happiness adds and multiplies as we divide it with others.

Promise-Prayer of Happiness

Lord, this is the day that you have made. I will rejoice and be glad in it.[1] The joy you impart to me is my strength,[2] and it enables me to rejoice always.[3] I rejoice in you, Father, because you have made me truly happy.

Thank you for enabling me to enter into your joy.[4] I will walk in the happiness you give to me throughout this day. Thank you for your Word which gives me abundant happiness, Lord. Because of your Word I have fullness of joy.[5]

The happiness you give leads me to love others, Father, and I want to love others throughout this day.[6] Because you first loved me I am happy, and it is your love for me that impels me to love others.[7] My heart is so full of happiness, Lord, that I constantly want to tell you how much I love you. Thank you, Father, for removing all fear from me and for giving me the spirit of power, love, and a sound mind.[8]

I trust you, Lord, and because I do, I rejoice in a wonderful feeling of happiness. I will ever shout for joy because of all you have done for me. You defend me, Father, and I love your name. You have blessed me so much, and your favor encompasses me like a shield.[9] Thank you for the blessing of happiness in my life, Lord.

References: (1) Psalms 118:24; (2) Nehemiah 8:10; (3) 1 Thessalonians 5:16; (4) Matthew 25:21; (5) John 15:11; (6) John 15:12; (7) 1 John 4:19; (8) 2 Timothy 1:7; (9) Psalms 5:11-12.

40. Healing

Key Promise: *"Beloved, I wish above all things that thou mayest prosper and be in health, even as thy soul prospereth" (3 John 2).*

The Psalmist gives us a wonderful prayer promise that emphasizes this truth: "O Lord my God, I cried unto thee, and thou hast healed me" (Ps. 30:2).

The Scriptures show us that God wants us to walk in good health. The Psalmist wrote, "Who forgiveth all thine iniquities; who healeth all thy diseases" (Ps. 103:3). He also gave us a promise that we can count on: "He healeth the broken in heart, and bindeth up their wounds" (Ps. 147:3). God promises to heal us when we are sick.

Jesus is the Great Physician of our souls and bodies. "With his stripes we are healed" (Isa. 53:5). The torture and death Jesus experienced on the cross for us enables us to receive the healing God has provided for His people.

In fact, it is the prayer of faith that heals the sick as James points out: "Is any sick among you? let him call for the elders of the church; and let them pray over him, anointing him with oil in the name of the Lord: And the prayer of faith shall save the sick, and the Lord shall raise him up" (James 5:14-15).

Promise-Prayer of Healing

Lord, I believe your Word which promises me that Jesus Christ is the same yesterday, today, and forever.[1] When He walked on earth, He went about all the cities and villages, teaching in the synagogues, and preaching the gospel of your kingdom. He also healed every sickness and disease among the people.[2] I believe He is still the same, and I know He wants to heal me when I am sick. Thank you, Father.

Heal me, O Lord, and I shall be healed; save me, and I shall be saved: for you are my praise.[3] I praise you, mighty Father. You forgive all my iniquities, and you heal all my diseases.[4] Thank you, Lord. When I am sick, you send your Word, and it heals me and delivers me from all destructions.[5] Your Word is life to me, and it brings healing to my flesh.[6] Thank you for the healing power of your Word, Father. I will never let it depart from my eyes. I will keep your Word deeply implanted within my heart.[7]

Praise your name, holy Father. I love you, and I thank you for healing me and keeping me in good health.

References: *(1) Hebrews 13:8; (2) Matthew 9:35; (3) Jeremiah 17:14; (4) Psalms 103:3; (5) Psalms 107:20; (6) Proverbs 4:22; (7) Proverbs 4:21.*

41. Heaven

Key promise: *"And God shall wipe away all tears from their eyes; and there shall be no more death, neither sorrow, nor crying, neither shall there be any more pain: for the former things are passed away"* (Rev. 21:4).

A heavenly home awaits every believer. Jesus promised, "Let not your heart be troubled: ye believe in God, believe also in me. In my Father's house are many mansions: if it were not so, I would have told you. I go to prepare a place for you. And if I go and prepare a place for you, I will come again, and receive you unto myself; that where I am, there ye may be also" (John 14:1-3).

Those who truly believe in heaven are the happiest people on earth because they are able to keep eternity's values in view and this enables them to avoid "sweating the small stuff." It is faith that builds the bridge from this life to the after-life.

There is only one road leading to heaven. Jesus said, "I am the way, the truth, and the life: no man cometh unto the Father, but by me" (John 14:6). Thomas Guthrie described heaven in glowingly vivid terms: "Heaven is the day of which grace is the dawn, the rich, ripe fruit of which grace is the lovely flower; the inner shrine of that most glorious temple to which grace forms the approach and outer court."

Thank God for the gift of heaven. It is our true home.

Promise-Prayer of Heaven

Heavenly Father, thank you for the promise of heaven. Even when I am persecuted for righteousness' sake, I can still be happy because I know heaven is my home.[1] Therefore, I am able to rejoice even in times of persecution because I know I will have my reward in heaven.[2] Thank you, Lord.

In heaven I have an enduring substance that is far better than anything this world has to offer.[3] I look forward to your promise of heaven being fulfilled in my life, Lord.[4] Now I see through a glass, darkly, but when I get to heaven I know I will see you face to face. Now I know in part, but then I will know even as I am known.[5] Thank you for all your promises, Lord.

How I praise you and rejoice, Father, over the fact that you have swallowed up death in victory. I look forward to the time when you will fulfill your promise to wipe all tears from the eyes of your people.[6] I know the truth of your Word which assures me that no one has ever fully heard or seen all that you have prepared for those who love you. I wait for the fulfillment of your promise, Father.[7]

References: *(1) Matthew 5:10; (2) Matthew 5:12; (3) Hebrews 10:34; (4) 2 Peter 3:13; (5) 1 Corinthians 13:12; (6) Isaiah 25:8; (7) 1 Corinthians 2:9.*

42. Help

Key Promise: *"God is our refuge and strength, a very present help in trouble. Therefore will not we fear, though the earth be removed, and though the mountains be carried into the midst of the sea"* (Ps. 46:1-2).

Jesus is our Helper in everything. We can do all things through Him because He strengthens us. (See Phil. 4:13.) He makes us more than conquerors. (See Rom. 8:37.)

Jesus is our Savior and Lord. He is the Helper of our bodies, souls, and spirits. He wants to help us at all times. He will never let us down.

Others may fail us, but Jesus never fails. Others may put us down, but Jesus lifts us up. Others may curse us, but Jesus always blesses us.

The Bible gives us many prayer promises which assure us that God is a very present help in our lives. One of these is found in 1 John 3:22: "And whatsoever we ask, we receive of him, because we keep his commandments, and do those things that are pleasing in his sight" (1 John 3:22).

Our God is able to help us with everything, in every way. Hallelujah! He will never let us down. He is always there, and He promises, "But my God shall supply all your need according to his riches in glory by Christ Jesus" (Phil. 4:19).

Promise-Prayer for Help

Lord God, you are everything to me. My spirit rejoices in you, my Savior.[1] Thank you for seeking me when I was lost and for finding me.[2] Thank you for choosing me to go forth and bear lasting fruit in your name.[3] Thank you for enabling me to bear fruit for you, Lord.[4] Without you, I can do nothing.[5]

You are good, O Lord, and you are always ready to forgive. Thank you for your plentiful mercy in my life which I always receive when I call upon you.[6] You are always there to help me; therefore, I will never be confounded. I have set my face like a flint, and I know that you will never let me be ashamed.[7]

You truly are a very present help to me, and I am receiving your help even now as I pray.[8] Thank you, Father. You are my refuge and strength, and because this is true, I will not fear anything or anyone.[9] You are in my midst, and I will not be moved. You are always there to help me speedily.[10] You are with me, Lord.[11] Knowing this, I will be still. I know that you are my God.[12] Thank you for your constant help in my life, Lord.

References: (1) Luke 1:47; (2) Luke 19:10; (3) John 15:16; (4) John 15:5; (5) John 15:5; (6) Psalms 86:5; (7) Isaiah 50:7; (8) Psalms 46:1; (9) Psalms 46:2; (10) Psalms 46:5; (11) Psalms 46:7; (12) Psalms 46:10.

43. Hope

Key Promise: *"For thou art my hope, O Lord God: thou art my trust from my youth"* (Ps. 71:5).

God has made many promises to us. Faith believes His promises. Hope anticipates the fulfillment of His promises, and patience quietly awaits the results. Faith, hope, and patience are core dimensions of praying God's promises.

Hope, like faith, sees the invisible, feels the intangible, and achieves the impossible. We cannot live without hope, because hope is the anchor of the soul, the stimulus to action, and the incentive to achievement.

Hope is faith holding out its hand in the dark, and it is putting faith to work when doubting might seem to be easier. Life with Christ is an endless hope, but life without Him leads to a hopeless end. Charles L. Allen reminds us, "When you say a situation or a person is hopeless, you are slamming the door in the face of God." With God, there are no hopeless situations or hopeless people.

Zechariah said we are ". . . prisoners of hope" (Zech. 9:12).

"Blessed is the man that trusteth in the Lord, and whose hope the Lord is" (Jer. 17:7).

Therefore, we must, "Hope to the end" (1 Pet. 1:13).

Promise-Prayer of Hope

Lord, I believe in the power of hope.[1] Thank you for imparting hope to me that keeps me from all shame.[2] You are the God of hope, and I ask you to fill me with all the joy and peace that comes from believing so that I will abound with hope through the power of your Holy Spirit.[3]

With your help, I will put on the breastplate of faith and love, and my helmet will be the hope of salvation.[4] Thank you, Father. Your great love for me has given me an everlasting consolation and good hope through grace.[5]

Therefore, I will lay hold upon the hope you have set before me. The hope you give is an anchor for my soul, and it is sure and steadfast.[6] Thank you, Father. Through your grace, I will hope to the very end.[7] I will hope continually, and I will praise you more and more.[8]

Because of the hope you give to me, I will no longer have to experience sadness or disquietude in any form. Instead, I will ever hope in you, O God. I will always praise you, because you are the health of my countenance, and you are my God.[9]

References: *(1) Romans 4:18; (2) Romans 5:5; (3) Romans 15:13; (4) 1 Thessalonians 5:8; (5) 2 Thessalonians 2:16; (6) Hebrews 6:18-19; (7) 1 Peter 1:13; (8) Psalms 71:14; (9) Psalms 42:11.*

44. Humility

Key Promise: *"Be clothed with humility: for God resisteth the proud, and giveth grace to the humble. Humble yourselves therefore under the mighty hand of God, that he may exalt you in due time"* (1 Pet. 5:5-6).

Jonathan Edwards wrote, "Nothing sets a person so much out of the devil's reach as humility." True self-knowledge leads us to humility, because when we see ourselves as we really are we realize how weak and needy we are, how much we need God in our lives.

Andrew Murray sums the matter up: "Humility is perfect quietness of heart. It is to have no trouble. It is never to be fretted or irritated or sore or disappointed. It is to expect nothing, to wonder at nothing that is done to me. It is to be at rest when nobody praises me and when I am blamed or despised. It is to have a blessed home in the Lord, where I can go in and shut the door and kneel to my Father in secret, and am at peace as in the deep sea of calmness when all around and above is trouble."

Now that's true humility, and it is an attainable condition in Christ. The Bible says, "Whosoever exalteth himself shall be abased; and he that humbleth himself shall be exalted" (Luke 14:11).

Promise-Prayer of Humility

Heavenly Father, thank you for helping me to find humility in my life. You have given grace to me in response to the humility you have imparted to me.[1] I fully realize that without Jesus I can do nothing,[2] and this is the key to humility in my life, Father.

I draw near to you now, Lord, and I know you are drawing near to me. I cleanse my hands of all defilement and I purify my heart as I humble myself in your sight. Thank you for lifting me up, Lord.[3] With your help, Father, I will serve you with all humility of mind.[4] In lowliness of mind I will esteem others as being better than myself.[5] I will not let anything I do be done through strife or vainglory, because I want to have the mind of Christ at all times.[6]

Help me, Father, to be clothed with humility because I know you give your grace to the humble. Therefore, I humble myself under your mighty hand, knowing that you will exalt me in your perfect timing. I cast all my cares upon you, because I know you care for me.[7]

Thank you for the power of humility in my life, Lord.

References: *(1) James 4:6; (2) John 15:5; (3) James 4:8-10; (4) Acts 20:19; (5) Philippians 2:3; (6) Philippians 2:5; (7) 1 Peter 5:5-7.*

45. Inheritance

Key Promise: *"In whom also we have obtained an inheritance, being predestinated according to the purpose of him who worketh all things after the counsel of his own will: That we should be to the praise of his glory, who first trusted in Christ" (Eph. 1:11-12).*

We are children of the King of kings, and our Father has promised us so many good things. In fact, our inheritance is in the form of all God's promises, and when we pray His promises we receive our inheritance from His hands.

Notice all that this inheritance entails: "Blessed be the God and Father of our Lord Jesus Christ, who hath blessed us with all spiritual blessings in heavenly places in Christ: According as he hath chosen us in him before the foundation of the world, that we should be holy and without blame before him in love: Having predestinated us unto the adoption of children by Jesus Christ to himself, according to the good pleasure of his will, to the praise of the glory of his grace, wherein he hath made us accepted in the beloved" (Eph. 1:3-6).

God has adopted us into His family. Therefore, all the rights and privileges of His family are ours. The inheritance He has bequeathed to His children is ours. All we have to do is to claim our inheritance by faith.

All of these promised blessings are ours in the here-and-now.

Promise-Prayer of Inheritance

Heavenly Father, thank you for the wonderful inheritance you have provided for me. You have opened my eyes, and you have turned me from darkness to light. You have delivered me from the power of Satan unto your power so that I received the forgiveness of my sins and the full inheritance of your children who are sanctified by faith.[1] Thank you for your Word which is my deed of inheritance.

I rejoice in the joyful certainty that all of your promises are for me. In fact, all your promises are yes and amen for me so that you would receive glory, Father.[2] Blessed be your name, Father. You are my God and Father, and you are the Father of my Lord and Savior Jesus Christ. According to your abundant mercy, you have begotten me unto a lively hope by the Resurrection of Jesus Christ from the dead. Now I enjoy an incorruptible and undefiled inheritance that will never fade away. Thank you for reserving that inheritance for me, Lord.[3]

By the promises of your Word I know that I am partaking of your divine nature.[4] Thank you for the riches of our inheritance in Christ Jesus.

References: (1) Acts 26:18; (2) 2 Corinthians 1:20; (3) 1 Peter 1:3-4; (4) 2 Peter 1:4.

46. Integrity

Key Promise: *"The integrity of the upright shall guide them" (Prov. 11:3).*

The dictionary defines integrity as: ". . . soundness; a firm adherence to a code of moral values, the quality or state of being complete or undivided." The word integrity implies honesty. Therefore, to walk in integrity one must walk in honesty and truth.

Integrity is the result of having our lives well-integrated around the truths of God's Word. The prophet Micah wrote, "He hath shewed thee, O man, what is good; and what doth the Lord require of thee, but to do justly, and to love mercy, and to walk humbly with thy God?" (Mic. 6:8).

A Psalm of David reveals the causes and effects of integrity in our lives: "Judge me, O Lord: for I have walked in mine integrity: I have trusted also in the Lord; therefore I shall not slide. Examine me, O Lord, and prove me; try my reins and my heart. For thy lovingkindness is before mine eyes: and I have walked in thy truth" (Ps. 26:1-3).

Integrity is a matter of truth, faith, and courage. It is strength and stability. It is unswerving adherence to the Word of God.

Promise-Prayer of Integrity

Lord, you have put integrity within my heart, and you have restored innocence to me.[1]

With your help, therefore, I will walk in integrity from this time forth. It is my heart's desire to be found blameless and upright, one who fears you and shuns evil. Help me to always hold fast to integrity in the face of all circumstances. Thank you for empowering me with your Word and Spirit which will enable me to hold fast to integrity, honesty and truth.

Let the integrity you give to me always be my guide.[2] Examine me, O Lord, and prove me; try my mind and my heart, for your lovingkindness is before my eyes, and I will walk in your truth.[3] With your help, Father, I will walk in integrity. Redeem me and be merciful to me as I strive to please you.[4]

O Lord, keep my soul and deliver me. Let me not be ashamed, for I put my total trust in you. Let your integrity and uprightness preserve me, for I wait on you. Redeem me, O God, out of all my troubles.[5] Be merciful to me, O Lord, and raise me up.[6]

References: *(1) Genesis 20:5-6; (2) Proverbs 11:3; (3) Psalms 26:1-3; (4) Psalms 26:11; (5) Psalms 25:20-22; (6) Psalms 41:10-12.*

47. Joy

Key Promise: *"The joy of the Lord is your strength"*
(Neh. 8:10).

Yes, the joy of the Lord is our strength, because
His joy is not based on external circumstances. It
comes from wellsprings deep within our souls.
His joy is never-ending. His joy stems from the
certain knowledge that God is working His
purposes out.

It is pure joy to realize these truths: "And
we know that all things work together for good to
them that love God, to them who are the called
according to his purpose" (Rom. 8:28). That's joy.
W.A. (Billy) Sunday said, "If you have no joy in
your religion, there's a leak in your Christianity
somewhere."

The Bible says, "These things have I spoken
unto you, that my joy might remain in you, and that
your joy might be full. This is my commandment,
That ye love one another, as I have loved you"
(John 15:11-12). Jesus is stating that His Word
brings joy to us, and the outgrowth of joy in our
lives is that we will love others in the same way
He has loved us.

Therefore, let us rejoice as we remember,
"This is the day which the Lord hath made; we
will rejoice and be glad in it" (Ps. 118:24).

Promise-Prayer of Joy

Lord, I thank you for your joy which is my strength.[1] When I come to the end of my journey, I look forward to your words, "Well done, thou good and faithful servant: thou hast been faithful over a few things, I will make thee ruler over many things: enter thou into the joy of thy Lord."[2]

Thank you for taking the spirit of fear away from me and replacing it with a spirit of power, love, and a sound mind that greatly produces joy in my innermost being.[3] I thank you that your kingdom does not consist of meat and drink, but of righteousness, peace, and joy in your Holy Spirit.[4]

Thank you for giving me a merry heart, Lord. I know that this will do me good like a medicine.[5] It also will give me a cheerful countenance which will help others to see your joy reflected in my life.[6] Thank you, Father.

God, you are my exceeding joy. Therefore, I will continually praise you.[7] In your presence is fullness of joy,[8] and I thank you for filling me with all joy and peace in believing.[9]

References: *(1) Nehemiah 8:10; (2) Matthew 25:21; (3) 2 Timothy 1:7; (4) Romans 14:17; (5) Proverbs 17:22; (6) Proverbs 15:13; (7) Psalms 43:4; (8) Psalms 16:11; (9) Romans 15:13.*

48. Justice

Key Promise: *"He is the Rock, his work is perfect: for all his ways are judgment: a God of truth and without iniquity, just and right is he" (Deut. 32:4).*

The justice of man pales in comparison with the justice of God which is always perfect, righteous, and devoid of error. God 's Word is the Law by which He judges, and His Word is perfect and complete.

G.K. Chesterton wrote, "Children are innocent and love justice, while most adults are wicked and prefer mercy." God wants us to be like children in the sense that we will love justice too.

God's justice is always tempered with mercy, but it remains justice nonetheless. Voltaire explains: "It seems clear to me that God designed us to live in society — just as He has given the bees the honey; and as our social system could not subsist without the sense of justice and injustice, He has given us the power to acquire that sense."

God is thoroughly just in all His dealings with mankind. Therefore, it is accurate to say that He is also fair. He has presented His law to us, and it is our choice whether to obey it or not. When we obey, we are blessed. When we disobey, negative consequences result.

Let justice prevail in our lives.

Promise-Prayer of Justice

Lord God, thank you for your justice which is perfect and without any partiality whatsoever. Help those who rule over people to be just as you are just.[1] Because your justice is so important and impartial, I ask that you would use me to lead people to know that you are our God, and that there is no other God. I want my heart to be perfect with you, Lord, so that I will always be careful to walk in your statutes and to keep all your commandments.[2]

Let your justice prevail, Father. The heavens are yours and so is the earth. You have established the world. Your arm is mighty, Lord. Your hand is strong. Justice and judgment are the habitation of your throne, and mercy and truth go before your face. Therefore, I will walk, O Lord, in the light of your countenance. I will rejoice in your name all day long. Your righteousness will exalt me, for you are the glory of my strength. You are my defense, O Lord. You are my King. I know you will always be fair and just in your dealings with me.[3]

Lord God, vengeance belongs to you. Lift up yourself, O Judge of the world. Render to the proud what they deserve.[4] You are a great God, and a great King above all gods.[5] Thank you for your justice, Father. Let your justice always prevail.

References: (1) 2 Samuel 23:3; (2) 1 Kings 8:60-61;
(3) Psalms 89:13-18; (4) Psalms 94:1-2; (5) Psalms 95:3.

49. Kindness

Key Promise: *"But thou art a God ready to pardon, gracious and merciful, slow to anger, and of great kindness, and forsookest them not" (Neh. 9:17).*

Kindness is a practical way to show forth love, as William Penn stated, "I expect to pass through life but once. If, therefore, there be any kindness I can show, or any good thing I can do to any fellow being, let me do it now, for I shall not pass this way again." Kindness, such as this, becomes a hallmark of the Christian life.

Kindness is a quality of life that is a natural outgrowth of the supernatural work of God's Holy Spirit in our lives. The Bible says, "But the fruit of the Spirit is love, joy, peace, longsuffering, gentleness, goodness, faith, meekness, temperance: against such there is no law" (Gal. 5:22-23).

Kind actions begin with kind thoughts, and the person who sows seeds of kindness enjoys a perpetual harvest. Someone has wisely observed, "The kindness you spread today will be gathered up and returned to you tomorrow." Kindness is a ministry that everyone can engage in, whether rich or poor, young or old. It is a ministry that needs no formal education or deep thinking, because it is a form of service to others.

Kindness is able to dry a tear and mend a broken heart. It is able to restore hope to a fallen soul. Henry Drummond wrote, "The greatest thing a man can do for his heavenly Father is to be kind to His other children."

Promise-Prayer of Kindness

Lord, through your love at work in my life, I will let my love for others be without hypocrisy. I will abhor all forms of evil, and cling to all that is good. Through your grace, Lord, I will be kindly affectionate toward others, with brotherly love. In honor, I will give preference to others. I will not lag in diligence, because I will remain fervent in spirit as I serve you. Continue to fill me with your hope, Father, so that I will rejoice and be patient in times of tribulation. It is my desire to continue steadfastly in prayer. Lead me to distribute to the needs of your saints and to show hospitality at every opportunity. I want to bless those who persecute me, Father. With your help, I will rejoice with those who rejoice and weep with those who weep.[1]

Help me, Lord, to be of the same mind toward others in your family. Keep me from setting my mind on high things. Lead me to associate with those who are humble. I never want to be wise in my own opinion, but I do ask for your wisdom to govern my life, Lord.[2]

Heavenly Father, when I see that my enemy is thirsty, lead me to give him something to drink. When my enemy is hungry, help me to feed him. Through your almighty power, I will never be overcome by evil, but I will overcome evil with good.[3] Thank you, Lord.

References: (1) *Romans 12:9-15;* (2) *Romans 12:16-19;* (3) *Romans 12:20-21.*

50. Kingdom of God

Key Promise: *"But seek ye first the kingdom of God, and his righteousness; and all these things shall be added unto you. Take therefore no thought for the morrow: for the morrow shall take thought for the things of itself. Sufficient unto the day is the evil thereof"* (Matt. 6:33-34).

The Kingdom of God is the Kingdom of heaven where our Father sits on His throne of grace, and it is also within our hearts. Paul wrote, "For the kingdom of God is not eating and drinking, but righteousness and peace and joy in the Holy Spirit" (Rom. 14:17, NKJV). That glorious kingdom exists within us, as Jesus stated: "The kingdom of God is within you" (Luke 17:21).

Jesus is the King of kings and the Lord of lords. (See Rev. 19:16.) His kingdom has come, is already here, and is yet to come. Jesus warned, "Repent, for the kingdom of heaven is at hand!" (Matt. 3:2, NKJV). He also said, "Thou art not far from the kingdom of God" (Mark 12:34). In contemplating the Kingdom of God it is important to remember that those who continue to engage in the works of the flesh, Paul said, ". . . [they] shall not inherit the kingdom of God" (Gal. 5:21).

In order to inherit the Kingdom of God, we must become like little children with regard to our ability to believe, trust, forgive, and obey. Jesus said, "Verily I say unto you, Except ye be converted, and become as little children, ye shall not enter into the kingdom of heaven. Whosoever therefore shall humble himself as this little child, the same is greatest in the kingdom of heaven" (Matt. 17:3-4).

Promise-Prayer of the Kingdom

Heavenly Father, I thank you that Jesus is the Lord of lords, and King of kings.[1] Thank you for buying me back from sin and Satan with the price of Christ's shed blood. Now I know that my body is the temple of your Holy Spirit who lives within me. I am no longer my own. I am a part of your kingdom, Father. Therefore, with your help, I will always endeavor to glorify you in my body and in my spirit because both are yours. Everything I am and have is yours as well.[2]

Father, I look forward to the time when Jesus will say to me, "Come, ye blessed of my Father, inherit the kingdom prepared for you from the foundation of the world."[3] Thank you for letting me enter your kingdom even while I am on earth and for the wonderful promise of your eternal kingdom in the hereafter.

I thank you, Father, that your kingdom does not consist of eating and drinking, but it is righteousness, joy, and peace through your Holy Spirit.[4] I receive the righteousness, peace, and joy that is being imparted by your Spirit into my life right now. This is truly heaven on earth to me, Father. Thank you for your kingdom.

References: *(1) Luke 6:46; (2) 1 Corinthians 6:19-20; (3) Matthew 25:34; (4) Romans 14:17.*

51. Liberty

Key Promise: *"And ye shall know the truth, and the truth shall make you free" (John 8:32).*

Jesus said, "If the Son therefore shall make you free, ye shall be free indeed" (John 8:36). Free from what, one may ask. The Bible gives us clear answers to this question. We are free from sin, corruption, and death. We are truly free.

The appropriate personal response to this freedom is outlined by Paul in his letter to the Galatians: "Stand fast therefore in the liberty wherewith Christ hath made us free, and be not entangled again with the yoke of bondage" (Gal. 5:1).

How do we find this freedom? Paul E. Scherer gives the biblical answer in no uncertain terms: "We find freedom when we find God; we lose it when we lose Him." It may seem ironic to some, but the greatest liberty we enjoy comes when we surrender everything to God. We are truly free when we become His bond-slave.

We enter into "the glorious liberty of the children of God" (Rom 8:21) when we surrender everything we are and have to God. Freedom is our birthright, but we find it only when we turn our lives over to our Creator.

Promise-Prayer of Liberty

Lord, thank you for making me free.[1] Your Word of truth has made me free.[2] There is, therefore, now no condemnation in my life. Through your grace, I will not walk according to the flesh any longer, but according to your Spirit. The law of your Spirit of life in Christ Jesus has made me free from the law of sin and death.[3]

I will walk according to your Spirit, Lord, and I know this will fulfill the righteous requirements of your law in my life.[4] Thank you for your Word which shows me how to set my mind on the things of your Spirit. As I do so, Lord, I am filled with your peace, because to be spiritually minded is life and peace.[5]

I look forward to the time, Father, when the creation itself will be delivered from the bondage of corruption, into the glorious liberty that all your children enjoy.[6] Through your Son, I am more than a conqueror, and I am persuaded that neither death nor life, nor angels nor principalities nor powers, nor things present nor things to come, nor height nor depth, nor any other created thing, shall be able to separate me from your love, Father.[7] This is true and glorious freedom for me.

References: (1) John 8:36; (2) John 8:32; (3) Romans 8:1-2; (4) Romans 8:4; (5) Romans 8:5-6; (6) Romans 8:21; (7) Romans 8:37-39.

52. Life

Key Promise: *"He that hath the Son hath life: and he that hath not the Son of God hath not life" (1 John 5:12).*

He who has the Son of God has life, but if we do not have Him, we do not have life. (See 1 John 5:12.) This refers to abundant life in the here-and-now, and it refers to eternal life in the hereafter. Jesus promised, "The thief cometh not, but for to steal, and to kill, and to destroy: I am come that they might have life, and that they might have it more abundantly" (John 10:10).

"The gift of God is eternal life" (Rom. 6:23). Because this is true, it behooves each of us to remember the words of William Penn: "The truest end of life is to know the life that never ends." Herman Melville expressed the same truth when he wrote, "Life's a voyage that's homeward bound."

Therefore, we must be faithful to God until the time of our deaths. The Bible says, "Be thou faithful unto death, and I will give thee a crown of life" (Rev. 2:10).

Praise God for the life He gives to us — it never ends!

Promise-Prayer of Life

Lord of life, thank you for your life-giving and life-sustaining Word which promises abundant life[1] and eternal life[2] to me. In Jesus Christ I have life, and His life within me is the light of mankind.[3] Heavenly Father, thank you for sending your only begotten Son to die on the cross for me so that I could receive eternal life.[4]

Thank you for your promise of abundant life.[5] For me to live is Christ, and to die is gain.[6] Father, it is my privilege to have been crucified with Christ; nevertheless I live, yet not I but Christ lives in me. Thank you for showing me that the life that I now live in the flesh I live by faith in your Son who loved me and gave himself for me.[7]

Hear my prayer, O Lord, and give ear unto my cry. Hold not your peace because of my tears, for I am a stranger and a sojourner on this planet. This world is not my home. Spare me so that I may recover my strength before I go on to the next life.[8] Teach me to number my days so that I will apply my heart unto your wisdom. Satisfy me early with your mercy so that I will rejoice and be glad throughout the life you've given to me.[9]

References: (1) John 10:10; (2) Romans 6:23; (3) John 1:4; (4) John 3:16; (5) John 10:10; (6) Philippians 1:21; (7) Galatians 2:20; (8) Psalms 39:12-13; (9) Psalms 90:12-13.

53. Light

Key Promise: *"The Lord is my light and my salvation; whom shall I fear? the Lord is the strength of my life; of whom shall I be afraid?" (Ps. 27:1-2).*

God is light, and in Him there is no darkness at all. The Apostle John wrote, "This then is the message which we have heard of him, and declare unto you, that God is light, and in him is no darkness at all. If we say that we have fellowship with him, and walk in darkness, we lie, and do not the truth: But if we walk in the light, as he is in the light, we have fellowship one with another, and the blood of Jesus Christ his Son cleanseth us from all sin" (1 John 1:5-7).

Jesus said, "Ye are the light of the world. A city that is set on an hill cannot be hid. Neither do men light a candle, and put it under a bushel, but on a candlestick; and it giveth light unto all that are in the house. Let your light so shine before men, that they may see your good works, and glorify your Father which is in heaven" (Matt. 5:14-15).

God's light has removed all darkness from our lives forever!

Promise-Prayer of Light

Thank you, Father, that in Christ I have life, and His life is my light.[1] When His light shines in the darkness, the darkness is not able to comprehend it,[2] but I thank you, Father, that you revealed the truth to me and set me free from all darkness.[3] Jesus is the Light of the world, and He is the true light that gives light to everyone who receives Him.[4]

Through your grace, I will walk as a child of the light in front of others.[5] I will have no fellowship with the unfruitful works of darkness, because I know that all things are made manifest by the light.[6] Therefore, I will expose the works of darkness wherever I go.

Thank you, Father, for the light of Jesus Christ who is the Light of the world. I will follow Him, and in so doing, I know I will never have to walk in darkness again. Thank you for the light of life He gives to me.[7]

The entrance of your Word gives me light,[8] and I will walk in the light of your Word wherever I go.[9] It was because Jesus came that my eyes were opened, Lord, and I thank you that He has enabled me to see your truth.[10]

References: (1) John 1:4; (2) John 1:5; (3) John 8:32; (4) John 1:9; (5) Ephesians 5:8; (6) Ephesians 5:13; (7) John 8:12; (8) Psalms 119:130; (9) Psalms 119:105; (10) John 9:39.

54. Love

Key Promise: *"There is no fear in love; but perfect love casteth out fear: because fear hath torment. He that feareth is not made perfect in love" (1 John 4:18).*

God is both light and love. Therefore, we should love one another. "Beloved, let us love one another: for love is of God; and every one that loveth is born of God, and knoweth God. He that loveth not knoweth not God; for God is love" (1 John 4:7-8).

Love is the most-excellent way. (See 1 Cor. 12:31.) Faith expressing itself through love is the only thing that really counts in this life. "For all the law is fulfilled in one word, even in this; Thou shalt love thy neighbour as thyself" (Gal. 5:14).

Love is perfection itself, and perfect love casts out all fear. (See 1 John 4:18.) It is also the bond of perfection, as Paul points out: "And above all these things put on charity [love], which is the bond of perfectness" (Col. 3:14). It is the glue that holds us to God, and it is the glue that holds us to one another.

"Love is the fulfilling of the law" (Rom. 13:10). All the Law is fulfilled by love. Samuel M. Shoemaker observed, "In the triangle of love between ourselves, God and other people, is found the secret of existence, and the best foretaste, I suspect, that we can have on earth of what heaven will probably be like."

Promise-Prayer of Love

Thank you, Father, for commending your love toward me in that while I was yet a sinner, Christ died for me.[1] Your amazing love for me was manifested when you sent your only begotten Son into the world so that I would be able to live through Him. This is true love, Lord, not that I loved you, but that you loved me first, and you sent your Son to be a sacrifice for my sins. Therefore, I will love others as you have loved me.[2]

I ask you, Father, to let Christ dwell in my heart by faith so that I will be rooted and grounded in your love. I want to be able to comprehend with all saints the height, depth, breadth, and length of your love. Help me to know the love of Christ which surpasses knowledge so that I will be filled with all your fullness, Father.[3] Fill me with your love.

Thank you for the certainty of faith that assures me that nothing shall ever separate me from your love which is in Christ Jesus, my Lord. I know that neither death nor life, nor angels, nor principalities, nor powers, nor present things, nor future things will ever be able to separate me from your love.[4]

References: *(1) Romans 5:8; (2) John 3:16-17; (3) Ephesians 3:17-19; (4) Romans 8:38-39.*

55. Mercy

Key Promise: *"O give thanks unto the Lord; for he is good; for his mercy endureth for ever"* (1 Chron. 16:34).

What is this quality we call mercy? It is certainly a divine attribute. Mercy involves compassion and forbearance that is shown especially to an offender. It is a blessing of charity, grace, and kindness. God sits upon the Mercy Seat — His heavenly throne from which He rules and judges.

Edwin Hubbell Chapin wrote, "Mercy among the virtues is like the moon among the stars, — not so sparkling and vivid as many, but dispensing a calm radiance that hallows the whole. It is the bow that rests upon the bosom of the cloud when the storm is past. It is the light that hovers above the judgment-seat."

Human mercy is a reflection of God's mercy in our lives. God wants us to be merciful, as Micah pointed out: "What doth the Lord require of thee, but to do justly, and to love mercy, and to walk humbly with thy God?" (Mic. 6:8).

God requires us to love mercy, and when we've experienced His mercy, it becomes so much easier to dispense mercy to others.

Promise-Prayer of Mercy

Thank you, Father, for always being merciful. You always give to your people, and you always bless our families.[1] Thank you for blessing me and mine with your mercy, Lord. You have shown great mercy to me, O Lord, according to your lovingkindness. Thank you for the multitude of your tender mercies in my life.[2]

I rejoice over the fact that your mercy is from everlasting to everlasting upon all those who fear you in a reverential way.[3] Lord, it was when I began to fear and reverence you that I experienced your mercy and you granted spiritual wisdom to me.[4] Now I know that your lovingkindness and your mercy are better than life to me.[5]

How precious is your mercy to me, Father. Because of it, I safely put my trust under the shadow of your wings. I am abundantly satisfied with the fullness of your house, and I thank you that you let me drink from the river of your pleasures. For with you is the fountain of life, and in your light shall I see light. Lord, continue your mercy and your lovingkindness in my life.[6] I love you, Father.

References: *(1) Psalms 37:26; (2) Psalms 51:1; (3) Psalms 103:17; (4) Psalms 111:10; (5) Psalms 63:3; (6) Psalms 36:7-10.*

Praying God's Promises

56. Might

Key Promise: *"That he would grant you, according to the riches of his glory, to be strengthened with might by his Spirit in the inner man" (Eph. 3:16).*

"There is no strength in unbelief. Even the unbelief of what is false is no source of might. It is the truth shining from behind that gives the strength to disbelieve," wrote George MacDonald, the Scottish preacher and writer. God is almighty, and this means that unlimited power is at His disposal. He is omnipotent — all-powerful. He is ". . . able to do exceedingly abundantly above all that we ask or think, according to the power that works in us" (Eph. 3:20, NKJV).

Human weakness can never be an excuse in a believer's life, because the Bible promises us that God will give power to the faint. Paul points out that God's ". . . strength is made perfect in weakness" (2 Cor. 12:9). A believer can no longer excuse his actions or his weakness by saying, "I'm only human," because the One who is perfect in every respect dwells within us. Jesus lives in our heart and He said, "All power is given unto me in heaven and in earth" (Matt. 28:18).

It is this knowledge that enables us to say, "I can do all things through Christ which strengtheneth me" (Phil. 4:13).

Promise-Prayer of Might

Lord, strengthen me according to your Word.[1] According to the riches of your glory, strengthen me with might by your Spirit within my inner being so that Christ will always dwell in my heart by faith and I will be rooted and grounded in your love.[2]

Strengthen me with all your might, Father, according to your glorious power, unto all patience and longsuffering with joyfulness. Thank you, Lord, for hearing my prayer and for making me a partaker of your inheritance along with all the saints in the light.[3]

You are my Rock and my fortress. You are my Deliverer. You are my God, my strength. I trust in you completely. You are my buckler, and the horn of my salvation. You are my high tower.[4]

Father, you have made it possible for me to be strong in you and in the power of your might.[5] Your Word is quick and powerful, and sharper than any two-edged sword. It pierces even to the dividing asunder of soul and spirit, and of the joints and marrow, and it is a discerner of the thoughts and intents of my heart.[6] Thank you for the might that your Word imparts to me, Lord.

References: (1) Psalms 119:28; (2) Ephesians 3:16-17; (3) Colossians 1:10-12; (4) Psalms 18:1-2; (5) Ephesians 6:10; (6) Hebrews 4:12.

57. Name of Jesus

Key Promise: *"If ye shall ask anything in my name, I will do it" (John 14:14).*

The name of Jesus is above every name. It speaks of the power and authority of God. To pray in His name is to pray with full assurance that everything His name represents will bring God's answers to our needs.

What a privilege it is to know that we can pray with His authority as it is represented by His name. At the mention of His name (when spoken in faith), the demons flee. Every knee shall bow at the mention of His name.

Six times in the gospels Jesus reiterated the importance of praying in His name. In His discourse on divine comfort He explained the reasons for doing so: "Verily, verily, I say unto you, He that believeth on me, the works that I do shall he do also; and greater works than these shall he do; because I go unto my Father. And whatsoever ye shall ask in my name, that will I do, that the Father may be glorified in the Son. If ye shall ask any thing in my name, I will do it" (John 14:12-14).

Andrew Murray wrote, "Our asking and the Father's giving are equal in the Name of Christ. Everything in prayer depends upon our comprehending this: 'In My name.'" Jesus said, "I have chosen you . . . that whatsoever ye shall ask of the Father in my name, He may give it you" (John 15:16).

Promise-Prayer in the Name of Jesus

Heavenly Father, thank you for the power of Jesus' name.[1] I know that whatever I ask for in His name, you will give to me. I will make my prayer requests in the name of Jesus, and I know I will receive your answers so that my joy may be full.[2]

Lord, I realize that praying in the name of Jesus is praying in the full knowledge of who Jesus is. Thank you for highly exalting Him and giving Him a name that is above every name, that at the name of Jesus every knee should bow and every tongue confess that He is Lord, to your glory, Father.[3]

He is the Rock upon whom the Church is built, and the gates of hell will never be able to prevail against it.[4] Jesus is my peace, my hope, my health, my all. He is my Rock of refuge, my high tower, my shield and buckler.[5]

My Jesus is your Word that became flesh and dwelt among us.[6] He is the Word of life.[7] He is Immanuel, and this means He is your fullness dwelling with us, Father.[8] He is the wonderful Counselor, the mighty God, the everlasting Father, the Prince of peace.[9] He is the Lily of the valley,[10] and the bright and morning star.[11]

References: *(1) Philippians 2:9-10; (2) John 16:23-24; (3) Philippians 2:9-11; (4) Matthew 16:18; (5) Psalms 18:1-2; (6) John 1:14; (7) John 1:1; (8) Isaiah 7:14; (9) Isaiah 9:6; (10) Song of Solomon 2:1; (11) Revelation 22:16.*

58. Newness of Life

Key Promise: *"Therefore if any man be in Christ, he is a new creature: old things are passed away; behold, all things are become new"* (2 Cor. 5:17).

Newness of life every day — that is the effect of God's promises in our lives. Someone has aptly stated, "Christianity is the land of new beginnings." Indeed, each new day is a whole new beginning with the Lord.

Paul wrote, "Therefore we are buried with him by baptism into death: that like as Christ was raised up from the dead by the glory of the Father, even so we also should walk in newness of life" (Rom. 6:4).

God makes all things new in our lives. He gives us a new song, a new purpose, a new direction, and a new perspective. He wants us to have abundant life, as Jesus pointed out, "The thief cometh not, but for to steal, and to kill, and to destroy: I am come that they might have life, and that they might have it more abundantly" (John 10:10).

The Bible says, "Behold, I make all things new. And he said unto me, Write: for these words are true and faithful. And he said unto me, It is done. I am Alpha and Omega, the beginning and the end. I will give unto him that is athirst of the fountain of the water of life freely. He that overcometh shall inherit all things; and I will be his God, and he shall be my son" (Rev. 21:5-7).

Promise-Prayer of Newness of Life

Father, thank you for the newness of life you've imparted to me. You truly have made all things new in my life[1] since that day when I first believed in your Son, my Lord and Savior Jesus Christ. You made me into a new creation. The old passed completely away, and all things became new to me.[2]

Thank you, Father, for delivering me from all bondage to the Law. Because you did so, I am able to serve you in newness of spirit, not in the oldness of the letter.[3] Therefore, I want to be your follower, Father. With your help, I will walk in love as Christ has loved me.[4]

By your mercies, Father, I present my body a living sacrifice to you. Make it holy and acceptable to you, because I know this is my reasonable service to you. Help me never again to be conformed to this world. Lord, I want to be transformed by the renewal of my mind so that I will be able to prove what is your good, acceptable, and perfect will.[5]

I love you, Lord, and I thank you for renewing me daily. I submit myself to your process of renewal at all times.

References: (1) Revelation 21:5; (2) 2 Corinthians 5:17; (3) Romans 7:6; (4) Ephesians 5:1-2; (5) Romans 12:1-2.

59. Obedience

Key Promise: *"Behold, I set before you this day a blessing and a curse; A blessing, if ye obey the commandments of the Lord your God, which I command you this day: And a curse, if ye will not obey the commandments of the Lord your God, but turn aside out of the way which I command you this day, to go after other gods, which ye have not known" (Deut. 11:26-28).*

The Bible clearly shows that God wants obedience from His children. "Obedience," Dwight L. Moody stated, "means marching right on whether we feel like it or not." Obedience is a key to great blessing in our lives.

Oswald Chambers wrote, "When God gives a vision, transact business on that line, no matter what it costs." Now that is true obedience. It is our duty to obey God's commands, not to direct His counsels. Every great person first learned how to obey, whom to obey, and when to obey. Christ was one child who knew more than His parents — yet He obeyed them, setting us a great and abiding example.

The Bible says, "Though he [Jesus] were a Son, yet learned he obedience by the things which he suffered; And being made perfect, he became the author of eternal salvation unto all them that obey him" (Heb. 5:8-9). Jesus learned to obey God through the things that He suffered, and He wants us to obey Him.

Promise-Prayer of Obedience

Heavenly Father, thank you for making it possible for me to obey you, and for all the promises of your Word which show me the blessings of an obedient life. Your Word tells me that if I will be willing and obedient, I shall eat of the good of the land.[1]

Help me to be obedient to your Word and to your will at all times, Father. Through your grace, I will obey you rather than men.[2] Teach me to obey all your commandments. I know it is true that obeying your voice is far better than any sacrifice because rebellion is as the sin of witchcraft in your sight, Lord, and stubbornness is as iniquity and idolatry.[3] May I never be found guilty of those sins, Father.

Thank you for all the promises of your Word, Father, which I know will come to pass as I learn to obey you. You have pointed out that if I love you, I will obey you.[4] I do love you, Lord, and I want to obey you in everything.

Your reassuring promises keep me going as I reflect on your Word which tells me that you love me. I know I am loved by you, Father, and I thank you for loving me and coming to me to take up your abode with me.[5] I know you are leading me into a life of complete obedience.

References: (1) *Isaiah 1:19; (2) Acts 5:29; (3) 1 Samuel 15:22-23; (4) John 14:15; (5) John 14:21, 23.*

60. Overcoming

Key Promise: *"Nay, in all these things we are more than conquerors through him that loved us"* (Rom. 8:37).

God has given us a way to overcome the power of the carnal mind. His Word promises, "I am crucified with Christ: nevertheless I live; yet not I, but Christ liveth in me: and the life which I now live in the flesh I live by the faith of the Son of God, who loved me, and gave himself for me" (Gal. 2:20).

God has given us a way to overcome the power of Satan. His Word promises, "Finally, my brethren, be strong in the Lord, and in the power of his might. Put on the whole armour of God, that ye may be able to stand against the wiles of the devil" (Eph. 6:10-11).

God has given us a way to overcome worldliness. His Word promises, "Whereby are given unto us exceeding great and precious promises: that by these ye might be partakers of the divine nature, having escaped the corruption that is in the world through lust" (2 Pet. 1:4).

God has given us a way to overcome pride. His Word promises, "But we have this treasure in earthen vessels, that the excellency of the power may be of God, and not of us" (2 Cor. 4:7).

God has given us a way to overcome despair. His Word promises, "And so, after he had patiently endured, he obtained the promise" (Heb. 6:15).

Promise-Prayer of Overcoming

Father, I thank you that you give power to the faint, and to those who seemingly have no strength, you increase their strength. I know that as I wait upon you, my strength will be renewed, and I will mount up with wings as eagles do. You give me overcoming power that enables me to keep on running the race you've set before me without becoming weary. You enable me to keep on walking without fainting.[1] Thank you, Father.

As I pray, I realize that you are filling me with all the joy and peace that comes through believing. Thank you for helping me to abound in hope through the power of your Holy Spirit.[2] Because you have given me the power to be an overcomer, Lord, I know I will inherit all the good things you have for me. You will always be my God, and I will be your child.[3]

My soul waits on you, Lord. I know your eye is ever upon me, because I hope in your mercy. You will deliver my soul from death, and you will help me to be an overcomer at all times, even during times of famine. You are my help and my shield. My heart rejoices in you, Lord, and I trust completely in your holy name. Let your mercy, O Lord, be upon me, according to the hope I have in you.[4]

References: (1) Isaiah 40:29-31; (2) Romans 15:13; (3) Revelation 21:7; (4) Psalms 33:18-22.

61. Patience

Key Promise: *"Now the God of patience and consolation grant you to be like-minded one toward another according to Christ Jesus: That ye may with one mind and one mouth glorify God, even the Father of our Lord Jesus Christ"* (Rom. 15:5).

The Bible says, "I waited patiently for the Lord; and he inclined unto me, and heard my cry. He brought me up also out of an horrible pit, out of the miry clay, and set my feet upon a rock, and established my goings. And he hath put a new song in my mouth, even praise unto our God: many shall see it, and fear, and shall trust in the Lord" (Ps. 40:1-3).

Patience, in the biblical sense, is waiting on the Lord. Patience stemming from faith enables us to inherit the wonderful promises of God. The Bible proclaims, "That ye be not slothful, but followers of them who through faith and patience inherit the promises" (Heb. 6:12).

At times, the waiting that is associated with patience may seem bitter, but at those times we need to remember that its fruit is sweet. Therefore, never think that God's seeming delays are His denials. Hold on. Hold fast. Hold out. He cannot and He will not fail you.

"For ye have need of patience, that, after ye have done the will of God, ye might receive the promise. For yet a little while, and he that shall come will come, and will not tarry" (Heb. 10:36-37).

Promise-Prayer of Patience

Heavenly Father, thank you for your exceeding great and precious promises that enable me to partake of your nature and to escape the corruption that is in this world through lust.[1] I rest in you, Lord, and wait patiently for you, because I know that those who wait upon you will inherit the earth.[2] Let me never be ashamed, Father. Show me your ways and teach me your paths. Lead me in your truth and teach me, for you are the God of my salvation, and I wait on you all day long.[3] Let integrity and uprightness preserve me, for I wait on you.[4]

Thank you for always being good to me, Lord. I will ever seek you as I hope in you and wait patiently for you.[5] My expectation is from you, Lord, because you alone are my rock and my salvation. You are my defense, and I will never be moved.[6]

My hope is in you, O Lord. Deliver me from all my transgressions. Don't let me be the reproach of the foolish.[7] I know, dear Father, that since the beginning of the world people have neither seen nor heard all that you have prepared for those who wait upon you.[8] I wait upon you, Father.

References: *(1) 2 Peter 1:4; (2) Psalms 37:7-9; (3) Psalms 25:3-5; (4) Psalms 25:21; (5) Lamentations 3:25-26; (6) Psalms 62:5-6; (7) Psalms 39:7-8; (8) Isaiah 64:4.*

62. Peace

Key Promise: *"Peace I leave with you, my peace I give unto you: not as the world giveth, give I unto you. Let not your heart be troubled, neither let it be afraid" (John 14:27).*

The way to find and keep peace is outlined for us by the Prophet Isaiah: "Thou wilt keep him in perfect peace, whose mind is stayed on thee: because he trusteth in thee" (Isa. 26:3). Dante Alighieri wrote, "In His will is our peace." We find God's will (and His peace) by staying grounded in the Scriptures, where we find His will for our lives.

One of the most peaceful thoughts in the entire world was written by the Apostle Paul: "And we know that all things work together for good to them that love God, to them who are the called according to his purpose" (Rom. 8:28). If we truly believe this promise and appropriate it for our daily living, we will know complete and abiding peace — "the peace of God, which passeth all understanding" (Phil. 4:7).

How can we have peace in this dark world of sin? Through the blood of Jesus Christ. The divine promise remains true: "The Lord will bless his people with peace" (Ps. 29:11).

Promise-Prayer of Peace

I love your Word, Father, and this brings great peace to my soul, because I know you have promised me that nothing shall be able to offend me.[1] Because you have given me peace, Lord, I will not worry, but in everything, by prayer and supplication, with thanksgiving, I will bring my requests before you. As I do so, your precious peace, which surpasses all understanding, keeps my heart and mind through Christ Jesus.[2]

Because you have justified me through faith, I now have peace with you, Father, through my Lord Jesus Christ.[3] Thank you so much for this gift of peace which is part of your kingdom-rule in my life. I praise you, Lord, that your kingdom does not consist of meat and drink, but it is righteousness, peace, and joy in the Holy Spirit.[4] Fill me with your Spirit, Father, so that I will bear the fruit of peace in all my relationships and responsibilities.[5]

God of hope, fill me with all the joy and peace that comes from believing your promises so that I will abound in hope and experience the power of your Holy Spirit in my life.[6]

References: *(1) Psalms 119:165; (2) Philippians 4:6-7; (3) Romans 5:1; (4) Romans 14:17-18; (5) Galatians 5:22; (6) Romans 15:13.*

63. Pleasing God

Key Promise: *"Ye shall walk after the Lord your God, and fear him, and keep his commandments, and obey his voice, and ye shall serve him, and cleave unto him" (Deut. 13:4).*

Trustful obedience to God, through faith, is the key to pleasing Him. Paul wrote, "I beseech you therefore, brethren, by the mercies of God, that ye present your bodies a living sacrifice, holy, acceptable unto God, which is your reasonable service. And be not conformed to this world: but be ye transformed by the renewing of your mind, that ye may prove what is that good, and acceptable, and perfect, will of God" (Rom. 12:1-2).

It pleases God when we give to Him all that we are and have. This is our reasonable service — a sacrifice that is truly reasonable in light of all God's mercies to us. The phrase "your reasonable service" has been paraphrased as "the least that you can do." Truly, giving our bodies, souls, spirits, and possessions to the Lord is the least we can do in light of all He has done for us.

What does God expect of His children? The Prophet Micah gives us a clear answer to this question: "He hath shewed thee, O man, what is good; and what doth the Lord require of thee, but to do justly, and to love mercy, and to walk humbly with thy God?" (Mic. 6:8).

Faith in God's Word enables us to comply with these expectations of our heavenly Father, and when we do so, we will be sure to please Him in all respects.

Promise-Prayer for Pleasing God

Dear heavenly Father, thank you for all you have done for me. I want to serve you and please you every moment of every day. As for me and my house, we will serve you.[1] Through your grace, Lord, I will not turn aside from following you. I want always to serve you with all my heart, because I know you will never forsake us. Realizing, Lord, that it pleased you to make me your child, I want you to know that I want to please you in every possible way.[2]

Help me to serve you, Father, with a perfect heart and a willing mind. Search my heart as I seek you. Thank you for the promise that I will always find you when I seek you with all my heart.[3] I will make a joyful noise unto you, O Lord, and I will serve you with gladness as I come before your presence with singing, and enter into your gates with thanksgiving. I go into your courts with praise, Father, because I am so thankful to you, and I will always bless your name.[4]

Help me to serve you and please you in newness of spirit, Lord, rather than in the oldness of the letter of the Law.[5] I will always pray in the name of Jesus Christ because I know that praying in His name brings your answers to me.[6] With your help, Father, I will keep your commandments because I love you so much.

References: (1) Joshua 24:15; (2) 1 Samuel 12:22; (3) 1 Chronicles 28:9; (4) Psalms 100; (5) Romans 7:6; (6) John 14:14.

64. Power

Key Promise: *"Strengthened with all might, according to his glorious power, unto all patience and longsuffering with joyfulness; Giving thanks unto the Father, which hath made us meet [able] to be partakers of the inheritance of the saints in light" (Col. 1:11-12).*

God's dynamic power is available to us through the Holy Spirit, the name of Jesus, the blood of Jesus Christ, and the Word of God. These sources of power enable us to face any situation with courage and confidence. They are sources of unlimited power, and we appropriate them through faith in God's Word.

"But ye shall receive power, after that the Holy Ghost is come upon you: and ye shall be witnesses unto me" (Acts 1:8).

"Wherefore God also hath highly exalted him, and given him a name which is above every name" (Phil. 2:9).

"And they overcame him by the blood of the lamb, and by the word of their testimony" (Rev. 12:11).

"For the word of God is quick, and powerful, and sharper than any twoedged sword" (Heb. 4:12). If we believe this fact then we will experience God's power, and His Word will keep us from sin. (See Ps. 119:11.)

Promise-Prayer for Power

Almighty God, thank you for the power you promise to me. Through faith, I appropriate your power in the here-and-now. Fill me with the power of your Spirit so that your name may be declared wherever I go.[1] I realize, Lord, that I cannot accomplish anything of lasting value in my own strength, but only through your Spirit.[2] Thank you for your promise that I can do and face all things through Christ who strengthens me.[3]

Thank you for sending your Holy Spirit to endue me with power from on high.[4] Through His power I will be a faithful witness for Christ.[5] I will never be ashamed to proclaim His gospel, Father, because I know it is your power unto salvation to every one who believes.[6]

Give me the spirit of wisdom and revelation in the knowledge of Christ. Give spiritual enlightenment to my eyes, Father, so that I will fully comprehend the hope of your calling in my life and so that I will see the riches of the glory of the inheritance you've given to me. Show me the exceeding greatness of your power as I believe your Word, according to the working of your mighty power in my life.[7] I love you, Lord.

References: *(1) Exodus 9:16; (2) Zechariah 4:6; (3) Philippians 4:13; (4) Luke 14:49; (5) Acts 1:8; (6) Romans 1;16; (7) Ephesians 1:17-19.*

65. Presence of God

Key Promise: *"My presence shall go with thee, and I will give thee rest" (Exod. 33:14).*

The key promise for presence of God gives us two promises in one: God's presence will go with us, and His presence will give us rest. It is possible to find a place in God where we are able to practice His presence every minute of every day. This is what Brother Lawrence reveals in his devotional classic, *Practicing the Presence of God*, and it is what Ruth Bell Graham alludes to when she put this sign over her kitchen sink: "Divine service conducted here three times a day."

The Bible gives us many promises about the presence of God. The Psalmist wrote, "God is our refuge and strength, a very present help in trouble" (Ps. 46:1). This knowledge causes him to proclaim, "Therefore will not we fear" (Ps. 46:2). When we realize all that God's presence in our life entails, we will be protected from all fear.

God promises, "I will never leave thee, nor forsake thee" (Heb. 13:5). Yes, His presence is with us always. This enables us to say, "The Lord is my helper, and I will not fear what man shall do unto me" (Heb. 13:6). When Jesus gave us His Great Commission, He concluded with these words: "Lo, I am with you alway, even unto the end of the world. Amen" (Matt. 28:20). The glorious truth is that He will be with us always. Hallelujah!

Promise-Prayer of God's Presence

Glory and honor are in your presence, Lord, and strength and gladness come from you.[1] You are showing me the path of life. In your presence there is fullness of joy, and at your right hand there are pleasures forevermore.[2] I want to learn to live fully in your presence each day, Lord.

I will ever sing to you, and make a joyful noise to you, because you are the Rock of my salvation. I come before your presence with thanksgiving and make a joyful noise to you with psalms because you are the great God, God of gods and King of Kings.[3] I serve you with gladness, Lord, and I enter your presence with singing because I know you are my God. You have made me, and I am but a sheep in your pasture. Therefore, I enter your gates with thanksgiving, and I go into your courts with praise. I am thankful to you and I bless your name. You are so good to me, Lord; your mercy is everlasting, and your truth endures to all generations.[4]

How sweet are the times of refreshing that come when I am restfully abiding in your wonderful presence, Lord.[5] Thank you for always being there.

References: *(1) 1 Chronicles 16:27; (2) Psalms 16:11; (3) Psalms 95:1-3; (4) Psalms 100; (5) Acts 3:19.*

66. Repentance

Key Promise: *"The Lord is not slack concerning his promise, as some men count slackness; but is longsuffering to usward, not willing that any should perish, but that all should come to repentance"* (2 Pet. 3:9).

Repentance is a gift of God. The Bible says, "And a servant of the Lord must not strive; but be gentle unto all men, apt to teach, patient, in meekness instructing those that oppose themselves; if God peradventure will give them repentance to the acknowledging of the truth; and that they may recover themselves out of the snare of the devil, who are taken captive by him at his will" (2 Tim 2:24-26).

To repent is to alter one's way of looking at life, and this alters one's behavior. It is to take God's point of view instead of our own. "True repentance," according to St. Ambrose, "is to cease from sin."

And for the repentant sinner it is pure joy, because the heavy burden of sin, guilt, and shame has been lifted. "Repent ye therefore, and be converted, that your sins may be blotted out" (Acts 3:19).

Promise-Prayer of Repentance

Lord God,[1] thank you for the promise of restoration that you give to those who fall.[2] Thank you for granting repentance to me,[3] for forgiving me of my sins, and for cleansing me of all unrighteousness.[4]

Because you have granted repentance to me, I know that there is, therefore, now no condemnation in my life. I choose to walk in your Spirit, Father, rather than walking after the flesh.[5] I now realize that to be spiritually minded is life and peace, but to be carnally minded is death.[6] Father, I want to be spiritually minded at all times.

As you remove the dross from my life, Lord, a vessel for the finer comes forth.[7] Therefore, with your help, I will speak the truth in love, and in so doing, I will grow up in all things.[8] Thank you for your goodness which leads me to repentance.[9] Because of your goodness to me, Lord, I now repent of the following sins: _____

_____

_____.

Thank you for hearing me, forgiving me, and cleansing me of all unrighteousness.[10] I believe the promises of your Word, Father.

References: *(1) Ezekiel 39:29; (2) Jeremiah 30:17; (3) 2 Timothy 2:25; (4) 1 John 1:9; (5) Romans 8:1-2; (6) Romans 8:6; (7) Proverbs 25:4; (8) Ephesians 4:15; (9) Romans 2:4; (10) 1 John 1:9.*

67. Righteousness

Key Promise: *"Blessed are they which do hunger and thirst after righteousness: for they shall be filled" (Matt. 5:6).*

Paul wrote, "Stand therefore, having your loins girt about with truth, and having on the breastplate of righteousness" (Eph. 6:14). The breastplate of righteousness that Paul refers to is a part of the armor of God that is given to us for purposes of spiritual warfare. The breastplate of righteousness protects our heart from being wounded.

Righteousness, therefore, is a gift of God. Jeremiah says that one of God's names is righteousness. "In his days Judah shall be saved, and Israel shall dwell safely; and this is his name whereby he shall be called, the Lord our righteousness" (Jer. 23:6).

The Lord's righteousness is imputed to us through faith. "For he hath made him [Jesus Christ] to be sin for us, who knew no sin; that we might be made the righteousness of God in him" (2 Cor. 5:21). What a glorious transaction that is! Jesus became sin so that we could become righteousness.

Believing and praying God's promises are keys to walking in His righteousness.

Promise-Prayer of Righteousness

Righteous Lord, I thank you for the promises of your Word. Help me to be a person of faith like Abraham was. Instead of staggering at your promises through unbelief, I want to believe each one, because I am fully persuaded that your promises will come true. Thank you for your Word which tells me that righteousness is imputed to me if I will simply believe in you as being the One who raised Jesus, my Lord, from the dead. You delivered Him to death for my sins, Father, and you raised Him again for my justification.[1] I thank you that I am justified by faith,[2] and this means you see me just as if I had never sinned. Hallelujah!

I praise you for your righteousness which delivers me from death.[3] Thank you for your promise, Lord, that you will not permit my soul to famish.[4] Instead, you promise that I will flourish like a palm tree and I will grow like a cedar in Lebanon.[5] Thank you, Father.

The work of your righteousness in my life is peace, and the effect of your righteousness in my life is quietness and assurance forever. Thank you for the peace, quietness, and assurance your righteousness gives to me, Lord.[6]

References: (1) Romans 4:20-25; (2) Romans 3:24; (3) Proverbs 10:2; (4) Proverbs 10:3; (5) Psalms 92:12; (6) Isaiah 32:17.

68. The Second Coming

Key Promise: *"Looking for that blessed hope, and the glorious appearing of the great God and our Saviour Jesus Christ" (Titus 2:13).*

Jesus is coming again! He promises, "And if I go and prepare a place for you, I will come again, and receive you unto myself; that where I am, there ye may be also" (John 14:3). Paul explains the Second Coming of Christ as follows: "For the Lord himself shall descend from heaven with a shout, with the voice of the archangel, and with the trump of God: and the dead in Christ shall rise first: Then we which are alive and remain shall be caught up together with them in the clouds, to meet the Lord in the air: and so shall we ever be with the Lord" (1 Thess. 4:16-17).

Paul then concludes, "Wherefore comfort one another with these words" (1 Thess 4:18). There is great comfort to be found in the knowledge of the Second Coming of our Lord and Savior. The truth of His promise to return keeps our hearts from being troubled and afraid. (See John 14:1.)

"Where is the promise of his coming . . . ? The Lord is not slack concerning his promise, as some men count slackness . . . . But the day of the Lord will come as a thief in the night . . ." (2 Pet. 3:4, 8-10).

Jesus said, "Surely I come quickly" (Rev. 22:20). "Even so, come, Lord Jesus" (Rev. 22:20).

Promise-Prayer for the Second Coming

Thank you, Father, for giving me the victory through my Lord Jesus Christ. I look forward to that blessed day when I will put on incorruption and immortality, because death has been swallowed up in victory. I know that you will change me in a moment, in the twinkling of an eye, at the last trump.[1] Thank you, Lord.

What a glorious day it will be when Jesus shall come again. Thank you, Father, for the wonderful promise that He will descend from heaven with a shout, with the voice of the archangel, and with your trump, O God. If I am alive at that moment, Lord, I know I will be caught up together with the dead in Christ who shall rise first, and I will meet my Lord and Savior in the air. You thrill me with this promise, Father, because it gives me hope and joy. How wonderful it is to know that you have made it possible for me to be with my Savior forever.[2]

Lord God, you have promised your children that when Jesus comes again we will be like Him, and this thought is incomprehensible to me now, but I believe it with all my heart. It gives me great hope, and I thank you that my hope in the Second Coming of Christ helps to purify me, even as He is pure.[3] Come quickly, Lord Jesus.[4]

References: (1) 1 Corinthians 15:51-57; (2) 1 Thessalonians 4:16-18; (3) 1 John 3:2-3; (4) Revelation 22:20.

69. Self-Control

Key Promise: *"But the fruit of the Spirit is love, joy, peace, longsuffering, gentleness, goodness, faith, meekness, temperance [self-control]:   against such there is no law" (Gal. 5:22-23).*

God is the blessed controller of all things, but He also wants to teach us how to exercise a measure of self-control in our lives as well, through the power of the Holy Spirit. Self-control entails temperance, moderation, and self-mastery.

Everything we are and have is God's in the first place, and this means that we are simply managers over everything God has given to us. As good stewards or managers, therefore, we need to be sure we exercise control over our minds, our attitudes, our behaviors, our finances, our families, our possessions, our bodies, and our appetites. This kind of self-control is possible through the power of the Holy Spirit.

Some philosophers have suggested that conquering kingdoms is easier than conquering ourselves. If we had to practice self-control purely in our own strength, we would surely fail. Our emotions might overwhelm us, and the appetites of the flesh might control us. Through the power of the Holy Spirit, however, we are able to gain control of our lives.

Promise-Prayer of Self-Control

Heavenly Father, help me to exercise greater self-control in every area of my life. I want to be a well-balanced Christian who follows your way in all things.

Through your grace, Lord, I will never again let my body, soul, or mind do whatever they want to do. Instead, through your strength, I will take charge of them. Help me to gird up the loins of my mind, to be sober, and to rest my hope securely upon the grace of Jesus Christ.[1]

I rejoice in your exceeding great and precious promises, Father, because they enable me to be a partaker of your divine nature and to escape the corruption that is in the world through lust. Therefore, with your help, I will give all diligence to add faith and knowledge to virtue in my life. To the knowledge your Word imparts to me I will add self-control, and to my self-control I will add patience. To the patience you impart to me I will add godliness, and to the godliness you impart to me I will add brotherly kindness. To brotherly kindness I will add love. Thank you, Father, that the end results of these processes will be fruitfulness in the knowledge of Jesus Christ.[2]

Thank you, Lord, for enabling me to practice self-control.

References: (1) 1 Peter 1:13; (2) 2 Peter 1:4-8.

70. A Sound Mind

Key Promise: *"For God hath not given us the spirit of fear; but of power, and of love, and of a sound mind"* (2 Tim. 1:7).

A sound mind is part of our rightful inheritance as children of the King. He promises, "Fear thou not; for I am with thee: be not dismayed; for I am thy God: I will strengthen thee; yea, I will help thee; yea, I will uphold thee with the right hand of my righteousness" (Isa. 41:10).

Soundness of mind comes to an individual when he or she has made peace with God, peace with others, and peace with oneself. All fear and worry interfere with soundness of mind. In His Word, God tells us, "Be careful for nothing; but in every thing by prayer and supplication with thanksgiving let your requests be made known unto God. And the peace of God, which passeth all understanding, shall keep your hearts and minds through Christ Jesus" (Phil. 4:6-7).

Soundness of mind is only possible as we think right thoughts. Sound thoughts help to produce a sound mind. The Bible says, "Finally, brethren, whatsoever things are true, whatsoever things are honest, whatsoever things are just, whatsoever things are pure, whatsoever things are lovely, whatsoever things are of good report; if there be any virtue, and if there be any praise, think on these things" (Phil. 4:8).

Promise-Prayer for a Sound Mind

Blessed are you, O God. You are the Father of my Lord and Savior, Jesus Christ, and you are the Father of mercies, and the God of all comfort. You comfort me, Father, in all my times of tribulation so that I will be able to comfort others who find themselves in various forms of trouble. Help me to comfort others with the same comfort you've extended to me.[1]

I am fully persuaded, Lord, that you will let nothing separate me from your love which I've found so completely in Christ Jesus. Thank you for the promises of your Word which assure me that neither death, nor life, nor angels, nor principalities, nor powers, nor things present, nor things to come, nor height, nor depth, nor any other creature, shall ever be able to separate me from your love.[2] Thank you, Father.

Through your power, Lord, I will never worry or experience anxiety in any form again. Instead, by prayer and supplication in everything, with thanksgiving, I will let my requests be made known to you. In so doing, I know your peace, which surpasses all understanding, will keep my heart and mind through Christ Jesus.[3] Thank you, Father, that you have not given me a spirit of fear, but of power, love, and a sound mind.[4]

References: (1) 2 Corinthians 1:3-4; (2) Romans 8:38-39; (3) Philippians 4:6-7; (4) 2 Timothy 1:7.

71. Stability

Key Promise: *"The eternal God is thy refuge, and underneath are the everlasting arms; and he shall thrust out the enemy from before thee; and shall say, Destroy them"* (Deut. 33:27).

As the gospel song tells us, "In times like these we need an anchor . . . . Your anchor holds beneath the solid Rock." That rock is Jesus and His Word. The Bible says, "Heaven and earth shall pass away, but my words shall not pass away" (Matt. 24:35). The Psalmist wrote, "For ever, O Lord, thy word is settled in heaven" (Ps. 119:89). The Prophet Isaiah concurred, "The grass withereth, the flower fadeth: but the word of our God shall stand for ever" (Isa. 40:8). Jesus proclaimed, "For verily I say unto you, Till heaven and earth pass, one jot or one tittle shall in no wise pass from the law, till all be fulfilled" (Matt. 5:18).

God's Word never fails, and that's why it is the key to stability in our lives. Its promises are the solid rock on which we should always take our stand. "Blessed be the Lord, that hath given rest unto his people Israel, according to all that he promised: there hath not failed one word of all his good promise" (1 Kings 8:56).

Christian stability keeps us during life's ups and downs, in and outs, highs and lows, overs and unders, because it is firmly planted, like a mighty oak, in the soil of God's Word. "But the word of the Lord endureth for ever. And this is the word which by the gospel is preached unto you" (1 Pet. 1:25).

Promise-Prayer of Stability

God, with your help, I will walk in emotional and spiritual stability at all times. I will attend to your words, Father, and incline my ear unto your sayings. I will not let your promises depart from my eyes; I will keep them in the midst of my heart, because I know they are life and health unto me.[1]

You have established me, Father. You brought me out of a horrible pit and lifted me out of the miry clay. Then you set my feet upon a rock, and you established all my goings.[2] Thank you, Father.

You are a very present help to me when I am in any sort of trouble.[3] Your name is a strong tower for me. It gives me a sense of peace to realize that I can find in your name the safety and stability I need at all times.[4]

Lord, thank you for your great faithfulness. I know you will keep on establishing me and keeping me from all evil.[5] Unto you, therefore, I pray, because I know you are able to keep me from falling. I know you will present me faultless before the presence of your glory with exceeding joy. You are the only wise God, my Savior, and unto you I give the glory, majesty, dominion, and power you deserve, both now and forever. In Jesus' name, Amen.[6]

References: (1) Proverbs 4:20-22; (2) Psalms 40:2; (3) Psalms 46:1; (4) Proverbs 18:10; (5) 2 Thessalonians 3:3; (6) Jude 24, 25.

72. Strength

Key Promise: *"That he would grant you, according to the riches of his glory, to be strengthened with might by his Spirit in the inner man; That Christ may dwell in your hearts by faith" (Eph. 3:16-17).*

God's strength is always available to us, but we must avail ourselves of that strength through faith in the promises of God, such as this one: "God is our refuge and strength, a very present help in trouble" (Ps. 46:1).

Alfred, Lord Tennyson wrote, "My strength is as the strength of ten, because my heart is pure." The purity and righteousness that are imparted to us by grace through faith help to make us strong enough to face whatever may come our way.

True spiritual strength realizes that nothing can happen to us that God and we cannot take care of together.

"Thy God hath commanded thy strength" (Ps. 68:28).

"Blessed is the man whose strength is in thee" (Ps. 84:5).

"My strength is made perfect in weakness" (2 Cor. 12:9).

Promise-Prayer of Strength

Almighty God, thank you for commanding strength for me, Father.[1] I realize, Lord, that all of my strength is in you.[2] I rejoice in the certain knowledge that, through Christ who strengthens me, I can do all things.[3] Thank you for your gift of wisdom which makes me strong, and the more knowledge I receive from your Word continues to increase my strength.[4]

You, Lord, are my light and my salvation; therefore, I know I have nothing to fear. Indeed, you are the strength of my life, and because this is absolutely true, I have no one and nothing to be afraid of.[5] Thank you for being my refuge and strength, Father. You are always a very present help in my life.[6]

Strengthen me, Lord, according to the power of your Word.[7] Help me to truly learn that strength will come to me as I quiet my heart and mind, for your Word assures me that in quietness and confidence I will gain your strength.[8] You always give power to the faint, Father, and you increase strength in those who have no might.[9]

Thank you for always empowering me with your strength, Lord.

References: (1) Psalms 68:28; (2) Psalms 84:5; (3) Philippians 4:13; (4) Proverbs 24:5; (5) Psalms 27:1; (6) Psalms 46:1; (7) Psalms 119:28; (8) Isaiah 30:15; (9) Isaiah 40:29.

73. Success

Key Promise: *"If the ax is dull, and one does not sharpen the edge, then he must use more strength; but wisdom brings success" (Eccles. 10:10, NKJV).*

The Bible outlines the pathway to success: "This book of the law shall not depart out of thy mouth; but thou shalt meditate therein day and night, that thou mayest observe to do according to all that is written therein: for then thou shalt make thy way prosperous, and then thou shalt have good success" (Josh. 1:8).

Successful living is a life-style that is based solidly upon the Word of God. It involves getting up every time we have been knocked down. The tools of success are faith and hard work. As Harvey A. Blodgett wrote, "The high road to success begins at your feet."

Erwing Lutzer wrote, "It is better to love God and die unknown than to love the world and be a hero; . . . better to have taken some risks and lost than to have done nothing and succeeded at it; . . . better to have lost some battles than to have retreated from the war; . . . What a tragedy to climb the ladder of success only to discover that the ladder was leaning against the wrong wall."

God, our heavenly Father, wants His children to be successful in every respect. That's why He's given us the promises of His Word. If we believe them and claim them and pray them we will be very successful indeed.

Promise-Prayer of Success

Lord, I believe it is your desire for me to walk in success. If I walk not in the counsel of the ungodly, but delight myself in your Word, I will be like a tree that is planted by the rivers of water, that brings forth its fruit in due season. My leaf shall not wither, and whatever I do shall prosper.[1]

Lord, you preserve the faithful and plentifully reward your children. Because of your faithfulness and love, I possess good courage and my heart is strengthened.[2]

Teach me to be faithful in all my responsibilities, Lord. Your Word teaches that a faithful person will abound with blessings[3] and good success. You are the vine, Lord, and I am simply one of your branches. I delight to abide in you and I rejoice over the fact that you abide in me. Help me to remember that abiding in you and your Word is the key to fruitfulness and success. Without you, I realize, I can do nothing.[4]

It is my heart-felt desire, Father, to hear you say to me, "Well done, thou good and faithful servant: thou hast been faithful over a few things, I will make thee ruler over many things: enter thou into the joy of thy Lord."[5] I want to always be your good and faithful servant, Lord.[6]

References: (1) *Psalms 1;* (2) *Psalms 31:23-24;* (3) *Proverbs 28:20;* (4) *John 15:4-5;* (5) *Matthew 25:21-23;* (6) *Luke 19:17.*

74. Thanksgiving

Key Promise: *"Know ye that the Lord he is God: it is he that hath made us, and not we ourselves; we are his people, and the sheep of his pasture. Enter into his gates with thanksgiving, and into his courts with praise: be thankful unto him, and bless his name"* (Ps. 100:3-4).

Thanksgiving is not just an act; it's a life-style. It's not what we have in our hands or pockets that should make us thankful, but what we have in our hearts. We should be thankful for the good things we have and, also, for the bad things we don't have. "It is a good thing to give thanks unto the Lord" (Ps. 92:1).

Jeremy Taylor wrote, "The private and personal blessings we enjoy, the blessings of protection, safeguard, liberty, and integrity, deserve the thanksgiving of a whole life."

John Henry Jowett wrote, "Life without thankfulness is devoid of love and passion. Hope without thankfulness is lacking in fine perception. Faith without thankfulness lacks strength and fortitude. Every virtue divorced from thankfulness is maimed and limps along the spiritual road."

Yes, thanksgiving is extremely important in the believer's life. Paul wrote, "Rejoice evermore. Pray without ceasing. In every thing give thanks: for this is the will of God in Christ Jesus concerning you" (1 Thess. 5:16-18).

Promise-Prayer of Thanksgiving

Father, thank you for everything, especially for the promises of your Word which enrich my life so fully. You have shown your greatness and your mighty hand to me.[1] My heart rejoices in you, Lord.[2] You are my rock and my fortress and my deliverer. You are the God of my strength, and I will trust in you. You are my shield and the horn of my salvation. You are my stronghold and my refuge. You are my Savior.[3] Thank you, Lord.

I gladly give thanks to you as I call upon your name. Help me to make your deeds known among the peoples.[4] I love to give thanks to you, Lord, for I know how good you are. Your wonderful mercy endures forever.[5]

I will praise you with all of my heart, Father. I will tell of your marvelous works. I am glad, and I rejoice in you. Therefore, I will ever sing praises to your name, O Most High.[6] I bless you, Lord. All that is within me blesses your holy name. I will never forget all your benefits to me. You forgive all my iniquities. You heal all my diseases. You have redeemed my life from destruction. You crown me with your lovingkindness and tender mercies. You satisfy my mouth with good things, and you renew my youth.[7] Thank you, wonderful Father.

References: (1) Deuteronomy 3:24; (2) 1 Samuel 2:1; (3) 2 Samuel 22:2; (4) 1 Chronicles 16:8-12; (5) 1 Chronicles 16:34; (6) Psalms 139:14; (7) Psalms 103:5.

75. Trust

Key Promise: *"Trust in the Lord with all thine heart; and lean not unto thine own understanding. In all thy ways acknowledge him, and he shall direct thy paths"* (Prov. 3:5-6).

Trusting in God is resting in Him. He is infinitely trustworthy, and His promises to us can always be counted on. John Wesley wrote, "It is a little thing to trust God as far as we can see Him, so far as the way lies open before us; but to trust in Him when we are hedged in on every side and can see no way to escape, this is good and acceptable with God."

Paul wrote, "There hath no temptation taken you but such as is common to man: but God is faithful, who will not suffer you to be tempted above that ye are able; but will with the temptation also make a way to escape, that ye may be able to bear it" (1 Cor. 10:13).

God is faithful, and the full realization of this fact comes by way of faith. Faith in the promises of God's Word leads us to trust the great Promise-keeper who always wants only the best for us.

Our Father is always with us. The knowledge of this truth wipes all fear away. Child-like trust is the deeper meaning of our faith. It is based on the promise given to us by the Psalmist: "I will fear no evil: for thou art with me" (Ps. 23:4).

Promise-Prayer of Trust

Heavenly Father, I trust you with everything I am and have. I know that every promise of your Word is worthy of my trust. Thank you, Lord.

Because my heart is fixed, trusting in you, I will not be afraid of any evil tidings.[1] I want to grow in my ability to trust you, because I know that true joy and blessing come from trusting in you with all my heart.[2]

You are so faithful to me, Lord. As I trust in you, I will continue in supplication and prayer both night and day.[3] Grant that I will never place my trust in uncertain riches or in any other thing, except you, the living God, who richly gives me all things to enjoy.[4]

As I learn to trust you, Father, I pray that you will help me to build other relationships in my life based on trust. All trust comes through Christ, and, as I turn toward you, I realize that I am not sufficient of myself in anything, but my sufficiency is of you, Lord, and I thank you that you have made me an able minister of your New Testament.[5]

I trust you with all my heart, Father.

References: (1) Psalms 112:7; (2) Proverbs 3:5-6; (3) 1 Timothy 5:5; (4) 1 Timothy 6:17-18; (5) 2 Corinthians 3:4-6.

76. Truth

Key Promise: *"And ye shall know the truth, and the truth shall make you free" (John 8:32).*

The truth of God's Word is the most liberating truth in the world. Abraham Lincoln observed, "The fact is that truth is your best friend, no matter what the circumstances are."

In the courts a witness promises to tell: ". . . the whole truth, nothing but the truth, so help me God." There is no truth in a half-truth. One of our main responsibilities as believers is to speak ". . . the truth in love, [so that we] may grow up into him in all things, which is the head, even Christ" (Eph. 4:15).

We are admonished in Scripture to: "Buy the truth, and sell it not" (Prov. 23:23). Helen Keller wrote, "Gradually I came to see that I could use the Bible, which had so baffled me, as an instrument for digging out precious truths, just as I could use my hindered, halting body for the high behests of my spirit."

The precious truths of God's Word are like nuggets of gold which we can mine at will. They truly make our lives richer. Each of God's promises is one of those truths.

The Bible says, "His truth shall be thy shield and buckler" (Ps. 91:4).

Promise-Prayer of Truth

Heavenly Father, thank you for your Word which is liberating me by its truths even as I pray. I thank you that your Spirit of truth is guiding me into all truth.[1] I praise you for the reality that Jesus is the way, the truth, and the life, and I know, Father, that I cannot possibly come to you except through Him.[2]

Because of these truths, I will put away all lying, and I will speak truth to everyone.[3] With your help, Lord, I will always speak the truth in love so that I may grow up into Christ in all things.[4]

I was brought forth in iniquity, and in sin my mother conceived me, but I know you desire truth in the inward parts, and in the hidden part you will make me to know wisdom. Thank you, Father. Purge me with hyssop, and I shall be clean; wash me, and I shall be whiter than snow. Make me to hear joy and gladness. Hide your face from my sins, and blot out all my iniquities. Create in me a clean heart, O God, and renew a steadfast spirit within me.[5]

The truth is, I need you, Lord, and I base my life on the truth of your Word. Thank you, Father, for setting me free through your truth.[6]

References: *(1) John 16:13; (2) John 14:6; (3) Ephesians 4:25; (4) Ephesians 4:15 (5) Psalms 51:5-10; (6) John 8:32.*

77. Understanding

Key Promise: *"But there is a spirit in man: and the inspiration of the Almighty giveth them understanding"* *(Job 32:8).*

In order to understand the promises of God we must approach them from a spiritual perspective. Paul wrote, "But the natural man receiveth not the things of the Spirit of God: for they are foolishness unto him: neither can he know them, because they are spiritually discerned" (1 Cor. 2:14-15).

The Bible tells us, "The fear of the Lord is the beginning of wisdom: a good understanding have all they that do his commandments: his praise endureth for ever" (Ps. 111:10). A reverential fear of God and an understanding of His commandments result in spiritual understanding and discernment in our lives.

The closer we get to God the closer we get to spiritual understanding because God proclaims, "Counsel is mine, and sound wisdom: I am understanding; I have strength" (Prov. 8:14). God is understanding. Without Him, there can be no spiritual understanding. Therefore, in order to get understanding we must get to know Him and His Word.

"Understanding is a wellspring of life unto him that hath it: but the instruction of fools is folly" (Prov. 16:22).

Promise-Prayer of Understanding

Heavenly Father, I seek your wisdom and your spiritual understanding for my life. Help me never to forget the understanding you impart to me. I will not forsake the understanding you give to me, because I know it will preserve me. In fact, I love the understanding your Word imparts to me, and I know it will keep me. Thank you for giving me spiritual wisdom and understanding, Father.[1]

Make me to understand the way of your precepts and promises, Lord, so that I will be better enabled to speak of all your wondrous works.[2] Give me understanding, and I shall keep your law. Truthfully, with your help, I will observe your law with my whole heart.[3] Your hands have made me and fashioned me. Give me understanding so that I may fully learn your commandments, Lord.[4] Through your commandments you have made me wiser than my enemies.[5] Hallelujah!

Through your precepts, Father, I get understanding and this causes me to hate every evil way.[6] Your Word is a lamp unto my feet and a light unto my path.[7] I am your servant, Lord. Give me understanding so that I will fully know and comprehend your testimonies.[8]

References: *(1) Proverbs 4:5-7; (2)Psalms 119:27; (3) Psalms 119:34; (4) Psalms 119:73; (5) Psalms 119:98; (6) Psalms 119:104; (7) Psalms 119:105; (8) Psalms 119:125.*

78. Victory

Key Promise: *"But thanks be to God, which giveth us the victory through our Lord Jesus Christ. Therefore, my beloved brethren, be ye stedfast, unmoveable, always abounding in the work of the Lord, forasmuch as ye know that your labour is not in vain in the Lord"* *(1 Cor. 15:57-58).*

The victory is already ours because of the cross of Calvary. It is a complete and total victory over sin, Satan, evil in all its forms, and death. Paul wrote, "Death is swallowed up in victory. O death, where is thy sting? O grave, where is thy victory? The sting of death is sin; and the strength of sin is the law. But thanks be to God, which giveth us the victory through our Lord Jesus Christ" (1 Cor. 15:54-57).

We appropriate this supernatural victory through faith. The Bible says, "For whatsoever is born of God overcometh the world: and this is the victory that overcometh the world, even our faith. Who is he that overcometh the world, but he that believeth that Jesus is the Son of God?" (1 John 5:4-5).

On the cross Jesus cried, "It is finished!" and this secured an eternal victory for all of those who place their faith in Him. Through faith, self-discipline, and the power of the Holy Spirit we are enabled to tap into vast resources of moral and spiritual power which make us victors, not victims.

Promise-Prayer of Victory

Thank you, Lord, for victory. Jesus' death on the cross and His resurrection from the grave assure me of victory in this life and in the life to come. I thank you that death no longer has any sting in my life, and the grave has no victory. Thanks be to you, Lord, because you have already given me the victory through my Lord Jesus Christ.[1]

The accuser of the brethren seeks to defeat me, but I rejoice in the certain knowledge that you have already defeated him. I now have victory over him through the blood of Jesus, and by the word of my testimony.[2]

Thank you, Father, for victory over every weakness and problem in my life. I will live and walk in the victory Jesus bought for me at so great a price. Forgive me, Lord, for the times when I've allowed circumstances and doubts to defeat me. I will always remember that it is faith that gives me the victory that overcomes the world.[3]

Because of the victory you purchased for me, Lord, with your continuing help in my life, I will be steadfast, unmoveable, always abounding in your work. I know that my labor will not be in vain because your victory upholds my life.[4] You have given me victory over every sin and temptation. Hallelujah!

References: (1) 1 Corinthians 15:55-58; (2) Revelation 12:10-12; (3) 1 John 5:4-5; (4) 1 Corinthians 15:58.

79. Wisdom

Key Promise: *"If any of you lack wisdom, let him ask of God, that giveth to all men liberally, and upbraideth not; and it shall be given him"* (James 1:5).

St. Augustine wrote, "The greatest good is wisdom." This statement is affirmed by the Word of God which tells us, "Wisdom is the principal thing; therefore get wisdom: and with all thy getting get understanding" (Prov. 4:7). The Bible also states, "Wisdom is better than rubies" (Prov. 8:11).

One reason why wisdom is so important and valuable is pointed out in the Bible: "Wisdom giveth life to them that have it" (Eccles. 7:12).

Wisdom comes from faith in God and the promises of His Word. Indeed, this wisdom He imparts to us defies definition due to its inherently spiritual understanding.

Heads that are filled with the knowledge of God and hearts that are filled with wisdom from God have little room left for conceit. You can pay for an education, but true wisdom is a gift from God. Therefore, wisdom is knowledge in action.

There is only one way to acquire wisdom, but when it comes to making a fool of oneself, an individual may choose several different routes.

"So teach us to number our days, that we may apply our hearts unto wisdom" (Ps. 90:12).

Promise-Prayer for Wisdom

Thank you for your Word, Father, for it gives knowledge, instruction, wisdom, and understanding to all who pay attention to its truths. You promise to impart wisdom to me if I will listen to your words and attain unto your wise counsels. I, therefore, enter your presence with trust, knowing that you will give me wisdom.[1]

Fill me with the spirit of wisdom so that I will be able to discern your will.[2] With you, Lord, there is both strength and wisdom.[3] Let my mouth speak your wisdom, Lord, because of the righteousness you have imparted to me.[4] In the hidden parts of my life, make me to know your wisdom.[5] Teach me to number my days, Lord, so that I will be careful to apply my heart to your wisdom.[6]

Your wisdom makes me happy, because the gain of it is better than fine gold. By wisdom you founded the earth, and by knowledge you established the heavens.[7]

Thank you for sending Jesus who represents your power and wisdom to us. Because I am in Him — and desire to always abide in Him — He has been made unto me wisdom, and righteousness, sanctification, and redemption. It is this reality that causes me to glory in you forever.[8]

References: (1) 2 Chronicles 1:10; (2) Exodus 28:3; (3) Job 12:13; (4) Psalms 37:30; (5) Psalms 51:6; (6) Psalms 90:12; (7) Proverbs 3:13-20; (8) 1 Corinthians 1:22-31.

• My Prayer Notes •

• My Prayer Notes •

• My Prayer Notes •

• My Prayer Notes •

• My Prayer Notes •

_____
_____
_____
_____
_____
_____
_____
_____
_____
_____
_____
_____
_____
_____
_____
_____
_____
_____
_____
_____
_____
_____
_____
_____
_____
_____
_____

• My Prayer Notes •